George Meredith, Bradley Gilman

The Pilgrim's Scrip

George Meredith, Bradley Gilman

The Pilgrim's Scrip

ISBN/EAN: 9783337290146

Printed in Europe, USA, Canada, Australia, Japan

Cover: Foto ©Lupo / pixelio.de

More available books at **www.hansebooks.com**

Popular Edition

OF

GEORGE MEREDITH'S WORKS.

Each Novel will be complete in One Volume.
Price, $1.50.

DIANA OF THE CROSSWAYS.
THE ORDEAL OF RICHARD FEVEREL.
EVAN HARRINGTON.
SANDRA BELLONI.
HARRY RICHMOND.
VITTORIA.
RHODA FLEMING.
BEAUCHAMP'S CAREER.
THE EGOIST.
THE SHAVING OF SHAGPAT, AND FARINA.

ROBERTS BROTHERS, Publishers.

THE PILGRIM'S SCRIP:

OR,

Wit and Wisdom

OF

GEORGE MEREDITH.

WITH SELECTIONS FROM HIS POETRY, AND AN INTRODUCTION.

Exclusive of the abstract sciences, the largest and worthiest portion of our knowledge consists in aphorisms; and the greatest of men is but an aphorism. — COLERIDGE, *Aids to Reflection.*

A composer of aphorisms can pluck blossoms from a razor-crop.
RICHARD FEVEREL.

BOSTON:
ROBERTS BROTHERS.
1888.

*O sir, the truth, the truth! is't in the skies,
Or in the grass, or in this heart of ours?
But O the truth, the truth! the many eyes
That look on it! the diverse things they see,
According to their thirst for fruit or flowers!
  Pass on; it is the truth seek we.*

FAIR LADIES IN REVOLT.

CONTENTS.

	PAGE
INTRODUCTION	vii
THE ORDEAL OF RICHARD FEVEREL	7
EVAN HARRINGTON	31
SANDRA BELLONI	43
RHODA FLEMING	55
VITTORIA	63
THE ADVENTURES OF HARRY RICHMOND	69
THE EGOIST	83
BEAUCHAMP'S CAREER	95
THE TRAGIC COMEDIANS	133
DIANA OF THE CROSSWAYS	141
THE HOUSE ON THE BEACH	175
VIGNETTES IN PROSE	179

Sonnets.

MY THEME	199
THE WORLD'S ADVANCE	200
THE DISCIPLINE OF WISDOM	200
APPRECIATION	201
EARTH'S SECRET	202
SENSE AND SPIRIT	203

Poems.

LOVE IN THE VALLEY	207
FRANCE. — DECEMBER, 1870	210
MEN AND MAN	223
THE WOODS OF WESTERMAIN	224
THE LARK ASCENDING	227
AUTUMN EVEN-SONG	229
BY THE ROSANNA	230
ODE TO THE SPIRIT OF EARTH IN AUTUMN	231
SPRING	236
MODERN LOVE	237
YOUNG REYNARD	241
MARTIN'S PUZZLE	242
INDEX	249

INTRODUCTION.

GEORGE MEREDITH.

BORN 1828.

INTRODUCTION.

IN a recent address delivered by John Morley, he laments the fact that the literature of Great Britain is singularly deficient in aphorisms. It is France whose writers excel in this branch of letters. When we think of *pensées*, adages, maxims, or epigrams, our minds turn instinctively to the names of Pascal, La Bruyère, Joubert, La Rochefoucauld, Joseph Roux, and Amiel. What English name could be placed in this category?

In this same address Mr. Morley alludes to "One living writer of genius who has given us a little sheaf of subtly pointed maxims in 'The Ordeal of Richard Feverel,'" and adds, " Perhaps he will one day divulge to the world the whole contents of Sir Austin Feverel's unpublished volume, 'The Pilgrim's Scrip.'" This writer of genius and author of the novel here mentioned is, we need hardly say, George Meredith; and his nine novels, after having hidden their light under a bushel for many years, are gradually finding their way to our library shelves, eventually to be given a place not very far from our honored George Eliot and our well-worn Thackeray.

A few years ago a copy of one of Meredith's novels was a rarity in this country; but now there are two complete new editions of his works; and, despite Mr. Meredith's own modest plea, "that the best of me is in my books," there are a large number of his admirers and friends who crave a less distant and more personal acquaintance with him. To meet this wish, and making use of all the material we could find, we have prepared this bare and inadequate sketch, humbly hoping that we shall not infringe upon the man's rightfully guarded personality.

George Meredith was born in Hampshire, in the year 1828. His parents died when he was quite young, and left him to be educated as a ward in Chancery. Of these parents little has been told the general public; but it is said that the blood of working ancestors flows in Meredith's veins, and perhaps this accounts for the sympathetic insight with which many of his homely characters are drawn. He received his early education in Germany, where he remained until fifteen years old. During these impressionable years German poetry, German music, German philosophy, and German humor all left their indelible stamp upon his youthful mind. It would be unjust to blame this foreign training for his faults of style, but it is not improbable that he first studied the art of fiction from Jean Paul Richter; certainly the strong philosophical and didactic note in all his literary work is distinctly Teutonic in origin. From Germany he was recalled to England by his guardian, who urged upon him the study of the law. This profession was distasteful to him, and he soon deserted it to give his undivided attention to literature.

His first published effort was an unsuccessful volume of poetry; then came " The Shaving of Shagpat," a series of fantastic tales, and "Farina," a short story. "The Ordeal of Richard Feverel," which appeared when he was twenty-seven years old, at once attracted the attention of one or two fair-minded critics in England, and since that time each new novel has gained for him a slowly widening circle of intelligent readers. No writer has fought harder for fame and fortune than George Meredith. His life in London for many years was a hand to hand struggle with poverty in its harshest forms. He found himself hampered at the threshold of his literary life with pecuniary difficulties, and with heavy debts not of his own contracting. For one entire year, it is said, he lived exclusively upon a diet of oatmeal. Beside this burden of debt, and the discouraging reception extended to the " firstlings of his muse," Mr. Meredith's early married life was fraught with much that was bitter. He married a daughter of Thomas Love Peacock, who is now remembered as an English humorist, author of "Headlong Hall" and "Crotchet Castle." His wife was a singularly brilliant and witty woman; and her death after twelve years of marriage closed a tragic chapter of his life, which he has never willingly opened even for friends to read. One son was the fruit of this union, who is said to have inherited some of his father's literary tastes, and now lives in Italy.

After a period of loneliness Mr. Meredith married again, and for many years lived a quiet, frugal, hardworking life with his second wife, in their pretty little cottage, which is situated at the foot of Box Hill, in one of the loveliest valleys of the Surrey Downs. But again, two years ago, Death came into his peaceful home, and again he was bereft of a most satisfying love. His second wife lies buried in the churchyard close by his cottage, and he speaks with quiet content of soon going to rest beside her. Two children, a daughter now about seventeen, and a son of two and twenty, who is an electrical engineer, still live with him. For the sake of this daughter, of whom Mr. Meredith is devotedly fond, he is now beginning to come out from his solitary retirement, and is occasionally present at social festivities. There is no dinner-table in the county where he is not a welcome and honoured guest. The novelist's home life is simple and frugal. He was at one time a vegetarian, and he rarely drinks wine except with guests. He dines contentedly on the plainest fare, and is personally indifferent to the material pleasures of life. "Contented poverty" he looks upon with great respect; and, as an author, he has never yielded a hair's breadth to the temptation of pandering to false literary taste for the sake of increasing his income.

George Meredith's cottage stands in a pretty garden upon the side of a hill. On a higher level within the garden he has built himself a little *chalet;* this contains only two rooms, a bedroom and a study, for his own private use, and stands under hanging woods on a terrace which commands a beautiful and far-reaching view of the neighbouring hills. Here, surrounded by his books, he spends his days, going down to the cottage about eleven o'clock for what takes the place of a mid-day meal; and again, between four and five o'clock in the afternoon, for a walk, which brings him home for dinner. He then remains with his family for an hour or two, returning to his solitude before ten o'clock to read until midnight. When guests stay at the cottage, as they often do, nothing in the usual routine is altered. But the host himself, and the kindly spirit of hospitality which pervades the home life, are the entertainment towards which every guest looks forward with happy expectation, and backward with pleasant memories. Then the talk is always interesting, sometimes brilliant; for Mr. Meredith is said to talk even better than he writes. The spontaneous charm of his speech cannot be caught on paper. The peculiarities of his style are modified, and much that is unpleasing when written down becomes agreeable in the wider range of spoken words. Links of meaning are supplied with sparkles all the brighter for the greater freedom. Face, gestures, laughter, and tones of voice, add a lucid commentary to the whole. When the guests are men, the evenings are finished upon the terrace of the study in fine weather, in the study itself in winter. Some especial literary work takes Mr. Meredith to London once a week. Then at the "Garrick Club" the talking parties are renewed. There the brilliant novelist is easily recognized as one of the best talkers of the day.

Nature gave George Meredith a robust and vigorous physique; but, partly by work, and partly by the experiments he is fond of trying upon his health, he has now become delicate, and in appearance he is described as seeming older than his years would indicate. In his younger days he was fond of walking, and he still enjoys a stretch over the downs. He used to say that he felt himself "pedestrian monarch of every country at which he looked." The Surrey Downs have been walked over and talked over by him hundreds of times.

Like most literary men, Mr. Meredith is an omnivorous reader, being catholic in his taste, and critical in his appreciation. He is a classical student, and has a wide acquaintance with the literature of many tongues. All the modern novelists of note, Tolstoi, Zola, Howells, Heyse, and George Eliot, he reads, considers, praises, and condemns, according as they seem to him to be deserving. He has a tenacious memory: a friend calls it "of iron, molten at the moment of impression, ever after cast in the form impressed." In regard to memory, Mr. Meredith himself asserts that it is all a question of heat: "If heat enough is excited by a fact, it will always be remembered." He quotes accurately from all authors, the known and the obscure; and his judgments of the minor authors are said to be peculiarly just and sympathetic.

In politics, as any reader of Mr. Meredith's novels knows, he is an extreme Radical. He does not believe in the advantages of a "church-ridden government." His religious attitude is one of profound reverence for the Maker of the Universe, and of unconcealed contempt for the makers of creeds and systems. In his own life, which has not been an easy one, he has worked out for himself a vigorous, inspiring, and spiritual faith. This shines through and lights up the pages of many of his novels, and the lines of many of his poems. At the age of sixty, after a life of deep experience, which has been furrowed by awful suffering, he can stand with head erect and heart still young, proclaiming that "There is nothing which the body suffers which the soul may not profit by."

It is because of the spiritual philosophy and golden wisdom of life with which not only "The Ordeal of Richard Feverel," but all of Meredith's books, are replete, that they deserve a permanent place in the literary world; they are collections of precious stones gathered from an experience which is world-wide. He is a coiner of brilliant phrases, which he throws at us with all the insolence of prodigality. His range of thought and reading has borne fruit in an abundance of maxims and epigrams, which extend from the homeliest truisms to the most original and profound reflections upon life and death. These aphorisms of Meredith differ greatly in length; and some are spun out inordinately, while others have that brevity which is the essence of the finest wit. At times we come across a saying as worldly wise as any of which Rochefoucauld was guilty, and, again, we find some deep truth, which seems to have been wrung out of a profound spiritual experience. The great Rochefoucauld revised some of his shortest sayings thirty times, while many we shall quote from this modern philosopher are, as it were, only rough outlines, — skeletons of great aphorisms which need to gather flesh and form, or more often to slough off morbid growth, before they can equal the perfectly symmetrical adages of the classical French school. A French epigram is never more than a half-truth, but it is so compact in form that every word tells. But many of Meredith's epigrams, although quite true, are enigmatical in form, and even justify that unfriendly definition of an aphorism as "A form of thought which wraps up something that is quite plain in words which make it wholly obscure." The French parish priest, Joseph Roux, says, tersely, that thoughts are fruits, and words are leaves. Now George Meredith offers us plenty of fruit, — an abundance of original thought, — but it is often hidden under foliage so luxuriant, that only after considerable effort do we come at it.

In each of his novels, this writer gives us, however, a number of short, brilliant sayings which have been skilfully hammered out of truth and experience. The parts of these sentences are like crystals, the particles grouping themselves together as if in obedience to an inner law. It is these sayings which stand out in our memories when we lay down George Meredith's novels; and it is these sayings which we have tried the experiment of excerpting.

Every author suffers more or less from being mutilated, and from having his thoughts considered apart from their organic relations. George Meredith himself says that "A gathering of all plums is not digestible;" and the great danger in making a book of excerpts is that readers will never discover that the author whose scattered and fragmentary thoughts they enjoy had any unity in his life's work. The selections gathered together in this small volume may prove that the writer of them can be witty, sarcastic, satirical, contemplative, paradoxical, and humorous; but that he is more than all these, more even than a great novelist and a clever poet, no one who does not read his complete published writings will ever be able adequately to appreciate. Those, however, who do study his novels conscientiously, — and they are novels which require study, — will find him ever emphasizing one great truth which is the very kernel of his life's work. This truth, this gospel, is contained in the following lines, which are quoted from a private letter written by Mr. Meredith to the compiler of this volume.

"I have written always with the perception that there is no life but of the spirit; that the concrete is the shadowy; yet that the way to spiritual life lies in the complete unfolding of the creature, not in the nipping of his passions. An outrage to nature helps to extinguish his light."

"To the flourishing of the spirit, then, through the healthy exercise of the senses," is the lesson we should learn from George Meredith. In his published works we find him again saying: "Our battle is ever between spirit and flesh, — spirit must lead flesh that it may live." "We have the power of resisting invasion of the poetic by the commonplace, the spirit by the blood, if we will." "The victory over the world, as over nature, is over self." "To have the sense of the eternal in life is a short flight for the soul. To have had it is the soul's vitality."

These quotations, and many more scattered throughout Mr. Meredith's prose writings, express the essence of his philosophy. In an interesting article written by his friend and neighbour, Flora Shaw, in the "New Princeton Review," in March, 1887, she quotes from him these words upon the subject of death: "It should be disregarded. Live in the spirit. Project your mind towards the minds of those whose presence you desire, and you will then live with them in absence and in death. Training ourselves to live in the Universal, we rise above the individual." Perhaps those often quoted lines from Browning, in "Rabbi Ben Ezra," may be said to contain Meredith's complete system of philosophy:

"Let us not always say,
 'Spite of this flesh to-day,
I strove, made head, gained ground upon the whole!'"
"As the bird sings and wings,
 Let us cry, 'All good things
Are ours, nor soul helps flesh more now than flesh helps soul.'"

Both Meredith and Browning recognize the full "value and significance of flesh." They are "human at the red-ripe of the heart," and are free from any taint of mediæval asceticism. They are rare examples of great spiritual teachers, who rejoice in the full development of the physical life. The spiritual life is the flower, and the roots of that flower must be firmly fixed in the earth, or the blossom will have neither strength nor beauty. Mr. Meredith's conception of the spiritual life is less tangible and less personal than that of Mr. Browning. The one is pantheistic, the other is Christian. The one recognizes a religion of law, the other one of love. The one is pre-eminently a philosopher, the other a prophet and a seer. No poet ever felt the "joy of earth," the beauty of the material universe, more fully than Meredith. He loves it, —

"With a love exceeding a simple love of things
That glide in grasses and rubble of woody wreck."

That same wild joy in living of which Browning writes so rapturously in "Saul," runs through many passages of Mr. Meredith's prose and poetry. He feels an especial kinship with nature, and learns his deepest lessons from the gathering clouds, the rich sunsets, the rosy dawn, and the tender hues of early spring. It is no theological, anthropomorphic, or even incarnate deity that brings Meredith strength and peace; but through the beauty and grandeur of nature he approaches the footstool of God.

Critics have often called George Meredith a cynic, and have complained of him for being sarcastic and satirical; they have even likened him to his own inhuman and odious creation, Adrien Harley; but he is cynical only as Browning and Clough are cynical, — as, indeed, all idealists are cynical, — that is, they have a conception of a perfect universe; the very grandeur of their conceptions makes the real world around them seem dwarfed and petty. At times, and in certain moods, they see nothing but the defects in human nature, just because their standard is superhuman; then the "spirit which denies" takes possession, and they groan and sneer; but this kind of cynicism is only a form of idealism; and not one of these poets is ever hopeless for the future of the race. Meredith sees the largest possibilities for humanity, if it will only subdue its passions and exalt its reason. According to Meredith's theory of life, "Reason, pure reason, is the only guide for man. It is our only means of spiritual progress." The grand mission of the poet and of the philosopher is to look forward hopefully for the spiritual progress of mankind; and it is with this class of writers that Meredith belongs. His cynicism is only occasional and superficial, one of the myriad moods to which all poetic minds are prone.

Among artists — and under this category we include poets, musicians, and men of letters — we find two broadly differentiated types. Those of one type produce their best work under intense excitement, when the creative impulse takes possession of them. They seem then to be controlled by some greater force than their own personality. But artists of the other type are always conscious of the laws of their art, and can easily subordinate their creative power to their reason. Granted, therefore, an equal amount of genius, and the nearest approach to perfection in style will be found in a writer who has learned to control his creative impulse and put it under the curb of his reason. Unfortunately, however, we rarely see this combination; the faultless writer lacks originality, and the original writer neglects style.

George Meredith is pre-eminently original; he has a vast ungoverned fury of creative energy; and his feelings are so tumultuous that he has no time to arrange or restrain the words which rush forth as if impelled by a torrent of emotion. The Italian expression, *con furia*, applies admirably to Meredith's prose style. Classical rules are nothing to him. He coins his own words, invents combinations, and is often guilty of forming the most outrageous sentences. His picturesque description of Carlyle's style is equally applicable to his own eccentric use of the English language: "A wind in the orchard style, that tumbled down here and there an appreciable fruit with uncouth bluster; sentences without commencement running to abrupt endings and smoke, like waves against a sea-wall, learned dictionary words giving a hand to street slang. All the pages in a breeze, the whole book producing a kind of electrical agitation in the mind and the joints." Carlyle's description of Richter's word-painting also applies to Meredith: "His language is Titanian, deep, strong, tumultuous, shining with a thousand hues, fused from a thousand elements, and winding in labyrinthine mazes." If the purest literary style be that of writers like Southey, where the reader can turn page after page without taking note of the medium of communication, then Richter, Carlyle, and Meredith, with their daring metaphors, pungent epigrams, and brilliant rhetoric, are only charlatans. But if style in literature be — like facial expression in a portrait, or atmosphere in a landscape — the strongest proof of the artist's individuality, then we can welcome the highly-coloured prose of Meredith, and delight in his fervid eloquence, without stopping to challenge him every time he steps aside from the commonplace and conventional. What Horace says of Pindar's style, may, we think, without sacrilege, be affirmed of Meredith's prose: —

> " Pindar, like torrent from the steep,
> Which, swollen with rain, its banks o'erflows,
> With mouth unfathomably deep,
> Foams, thunders, glows."

When we turn from considering Mr. Meredith's prose style to considering his poetry, we naturally expect his gift of language, his fertile fancy, and his spontaneity to be also characteristics of his verse. Mr. Meredith's prose is the prose of a poet; but where in his poetry do we find that exquisite lyrical touch which delighted us in passages of "Richard Feverel" and "Beauchamp's Career"? There is an odd mixture of the poet and the philosopher in Meredith's mental make-up; in his poetry the philosophic element is obtrusive. The didactic instinct — that fatal pedagogic hand which has strangled the muse of many a poet — claims him, and forces him to descend from Mount Parnassus and take possession of the schoolmaster's chair. It is easy to recall occasional lines in "The Woods of Westermain" which are melodious; there is also a succession of enchanting fancies in "Love in the Valley," and some of its verses are as graceful and unfettered as the joyous carolling of song-birds; but a poet must be judged by the mass of his work, and by far the largest part of Mr. Meredith's verse is harsh, uncouth, and scarcely intelligible. Take such lines as these :—

> "Still he heard, and dog-like, hog-like, ran,
> Nose of hearing till his blind sight saw
> Woman stood with man
> Mouthing low at paw."

Does the reader think this deserves the name of poetry? Or, take the poem called "The Last Contention," in which Mr. Meredith describes the young soul hampered by the aged body! It is a remarkable poem, and the conception is entirely original, but how involved and fantastic is the phraseology, and how unlovely is the metaphor!

> " Young captain of a crazy bark,
> O tameless heart in battered frame!"

An audacity that many critics claim to be wholly affected, is one of the strongest peculiarities of Meredith's poetry. Instead of remodelling his style to suit the taste of the critics, who fell upon his first volume of verse like wolves and tore it to shreds, we can fancy the indignant poet, like his own creation, Diana, in "a fit of angry cynicism composing phrases as baits for critics to quote condemnatory of the attractiveness of the work." The sonnet called "The Point of Taste" bears marks of having been written when Mr. Meredith's ire had been roused by the injustice of contemporary criticism :—

> "Unhappy poets of a sunken prime!
> You to reviewers are as ball to bat.
> They shadow you with Homer, knock you flat
> With Shakespeare; bludgeons brainingly sublime
> On you the excommunicates of Rhyme
> Because you sing not in the living fat,
> The wiry whiz of an intrusive gnat
> Is verse that shuns their self-producing time.
> Sound them their clocks with loud alarum trump,
> Or watches ticking temporal at their fobs,
> You win their pleased attention. But, bright God
> O' the lyre, what bully-drawlers they applaud!
> Rather for us a tavern-catch and bump
> Chorus, where Lumpkin with his Giles hobnobs."

INTRODUCTION.

No one can wonder that the author of that great heart-tragedy, "Modern Love," should have been indignant at seeing the tinkling verses of mediocre poetasters, and sentimental dilettanti, preferred to his own; for the author of "Martin's Puzzle," "Love in a Valley," "Melampus," "The Lark Ascending," and that grand, impassioned "Ode to France," had the melodic faculty when he chose to use it. It would be the greatest possible advantage to Mr. Meredith's poetical reputation if some sympathetic critic would collect his best poems, and let the public judge of them apart from his worst. The collection would be small, — and a few of these best poems we include in this volume of excerpts, — but, taken altogether, it would show the author's poetic possibilities.

The poet Meredith's aim, according to his own definition, has been to utter "the truthful in a tuneful way." But the tuneful he has always willingly sacrificed to the truthful; which accounts for many of his poetic failures. Perhaps, had Meredith persisted in his poetical work and defied adverse criticism, as did Browning, he might to-day have shared Browning's long delayed laurels. Certainly the two men have much in common; the same psychological problems interest them, and the same strong human emotions stir them. Vigorous intellectuality and rude strength are the salient features of their poetry; and either is always ready to sacrifice beauty to truth, form to fact. It is not so much "born poets" as poetic thinkers that will appreciate the best of Meredith's poetry; and is not this true also of Browning's poetry?

The poetry of neither of these writers is "Meat for little people or for fools." It is only for those who crave and can digest a stimulating intellectual diet. For such, and for such only, some of Mr. Meredith's poems will be a revelation, and will teach a lofty and spiritual philosophy. "Great thoughts insure musical expression," Emerson says; and we can easily imagine the saying falling from Meredith's lips. Beautiful expression is something he never seeks for itself; if the impression is exquisite, the expression will take care of itself; the imagination awakened will bring its own language. This is the theory of one who has been sometimes called "the Inarticulate Poet." There are lines, however, — such as the description of Spring from "Grandfather Bridgeman," — which have a delicate lyrical grace, and show Meredith's capacity for the purest poetic work. These bewitching lines prove that he was born with the poet's eye and ear: —

"The day was a van-bird of summer; the robin still piped, but the blue,
 A warm and dreamy palace with voices of larks ringing through,
 Looked down as if wistfully eying the blossoms that fell from its lap;
 A day to sweeten the juices, — a day to quicken the sap!
 All round the shadowy orchard sloped meadows in gold, and the dear
 Shy violets breathed their hearts out, — the maiden breath of the year!"

Meredith, however, deems the philosopher's mission to be the nobler. Power he thinks has not been given us for pleasure only. The work of the prophet is above that of the poet. Until, therefore, we appreciate this writer's deep sense of his responsibility as a teacher we shall not understand either his fiction or his poetry. He loves Nature passionately, but he writes of her in order to show that "she can lead us, only she, unto God's footstool, whither she reaches." Meredith's vein of philosophy is like a musical theme, often concealed, but always to be discovered underlying every portion of his literary work. The great Apostle to the Gentiles never preached more earnestly that "to be carnally minded is death, but to be spiritually minded is life and peace," than does this nineteenth century preacher, who, whether in poetry or in prose, is always hurling anathemas at the corruptions, the shams, and the sentimentalities of the age. If Mr. Meredith's philosophy is like a musical theme, his character and life form a most noble accompaniment. Who can look at his intellectual, delicately cut, and highly spiritual face, without feeling sure that he is one of those who, "after great tribulation, have overcome the world"? In his own life George Meredith has proved the greatest and most prominent tenet of his philosophy, — that it is possible to rise above the temporal and personal, however dark and painful it may be, and to live wholly, and even joyfully, in the Universal and Eternal.

As we turn now to consider impartially the place of

Mr. Meredith as a novelist, we must remember that none of his novels, however much they may be admired by a few, have ever attained what can be called general popularity. For nearly fifty years "The Ordeal of Richard Feverel" was a forgotten book; and neither "Beauchamp's Career" nor "The Egoist" made more than a fleeting impression on literary London at the time of its first publication. If we stop to seek the reason for this strange neglect, we find ourselves forced to the opinion that Meredith wrote over the heads of most readers. He would not make any concessions to the weaknesses of his public. "Of me and of my theme think what thou wilt!"—he wrote proudly. He was content to impress selected minds, and to enjoy the special function of the great man's intellect, which, according to Walter Savage Landor, "puts in motion the intellect of others." There are two requirements which Mr. Meredith makes of his readers: first, that they shall approach his novels with intelligent and wide-awake minds; and secondly, that they shall not shrink from facing and acknowledging the sternest facts of life. Now most habitual novel readers are not intelligent; they have weakened their minds by living upon what Carlyle calls sarcastically "pap and treacle fiction"; and they are utterly unable to read any book which requires concentration of their intellectual faculties. Then, among intelligent readers, there is a large class who refuse to look at the unpleasant side of life; who positively decline to read any book in which the sins of men and women are exposed unvarnished to their gaze. By such readers — and there are many such — "Anna Karénina" is condemned, and "The Ordeal of Richard Feverel" is considered unendurable. Moreover, some critics and devourers of sentimental fiction often fail to perceive a difference between a great philosophical novel with a distinct moral purpose, and the worst examples of French realistic fiction. That a writer touches upon the awful subject of illicit love is sufficient to condemn him in prudish eyes; and the fact that he draws a terrible lesson from its portrayal does not, for them, redeem his book. Accordingly, Meredith's courageous and almost coarse treatment of sin in "The Ordeal of Richard Feverel" and "Rhoda Fleming" has closed these novels for all readers who refuse to look outside their own narrow circle of experience into the broader field of the world's temptations and moral strifes. Thus, at the beginning, these novels were ruled out by the subscribers to Mudie's library, and were kept from the inevitable approval of the more cultivated novel reader. "The Ordeal of Richard Feverel" was not sentimental enough to draw largely for its readers from London boudoirs; it was not immoral enough, and required too much mental exertion, to find immediate readers in the clubs and the mess-rooms.

Judged from the standpoint of literary excellence, "The Ordeal of Richard Feverel" is the most artistic of all Meredith's books. It is greater as a whole, and it is greater in each of its parts. In it the reader is called upon to explore the depths of life; and perhaps no young person puts down this sad portrayal of temptation, sin, and suffering with exactly the same views of human nature he held when he took it up. Parts of the book show intense dramatic power, and some passages and scenes are lyrical masterpieces. Who, that has read it, will ever forget that exquisite description of the gentle Lucy, Richard's girl-wife! Or what cynic in fiction is as subtlely satanic as Adrian Harley! Above all, what a capacity for analysis is shown in the character of the unconscious hypocrite, Sir Austin Feverel! It is in the grouping of these characters, also, that a master's hand is shown. They are arranged as skilfully as tableaux, — the author bearing in mind not only each character by itself, but each in relation to all the other groups. There are two remarkable scenes in "The Ordeal of Richard Feverel," which no sensitive reader can forget. Robert Louis Stevenson does not hesitate to pronounce one of them — the final interview between Lucy and Richard Feverel — to be "the strongest scene, since Shakespeare, in the English tongue." The other scene, the first meeting by the river, is very different from this, but equally great; it is pure romance, and idyllic in its sweetness; it is the most thrilling, enchanting love-scene ever described by any English novelist; and it lingers in the memory as linger musical passages in Browning's "Blot on the 'Scutcheon," or sweet melodies from the German Folk-Songs. It is far superior to any love-scene in George Eliot or

Thackeray; for it contains the essence of first love in its purest, most ideal form, — first love as it should come once into the life of every human being.

Besides these two intense scenes, the one joyous, the other tragic, this novel is surcharged with aphorisms; it is a necklace of rich gems in which jewels of all kinds find place; sudden meteors of thought, comet-like flashes of wit, keen shafts of satire, and bursts of melodious rhetoric, compose the brilliant background of the novel; and against this, aided by it, the well-meaning but mistaken Bennet, the tender Lucy, the fair Lady Blandish, and the stormy Richard act out the dramas of their eventful lives. What a wonderful spectacle of life is "The Ordeal of Richard Feverel"! It is not only a work of genius, but a great moral tragedy; and it cannot fail to make an indelible impression upon the mind of every thoughtful reader.

It is only after we have exhausted the short walks in our neighborhood, where the paths are already cleared, that we attempt the more distant excursions, and cut our way through bush and bramble; so it is that, after we have enjoyed George Eliot's smooth English style, and Thackeray's simple conversational form of narrative, we shall feel tempted to break through the rough and tortuous sentences of George Meredith. But the effort once made, the rough pathway is soon forgotten, and we are amply repaid by the beauty of the landscape. The first steps demanded in overcoming the peculiar difficulties of Meredith's style require concentration and perseverance; but, these once taken, the reader becomes absorbed in the powerful and impressive soul-dramas which the great novelist creates and exhibits with such marvellous power.

"The Shaving of Shagpat," that strange web of Eastern fancies, was published in 1855, and was Meredith's first prose work. Next came "The Ordeal of Richard Feverel," in 1859, and in 1861 appeared "Evan Harrington." The contrast between "The Ordeal of Richard Feverel" and "Evan Harrington" is marked. For the first novel is a tragedy, and stirs our deepest and saddest emotions; the second novel is a comedy, and amuses us by making the antics of the human animals seem outrageously comic and absurd. "Evan Harrington" is devoted to portraying the vices and follies of fashionable life, and the particularly amusing vicissitudes of the Harrington family. The hero of the book, Evan, was the son of "Old Mel," a fashionable tailor; and the efforts made by his sister, the Portuguese Countess de Saldas, to conceal her father's profession, and to assist her brother to make a good marriage, are described with delicious humour. The character of the scheming Countess is drawn with immense skill, and even suggests that queen of adventuresses, Becky Sharp; but "Vanity Fair" is a satire, while "Evan Harrington" is an extravaganza; in the one novel real people walk and talk much as they do in life; in the other, the characters are all exaggerated, painted in broad scenic colors; they

Thackeray; for it contains the essence of first love in its purest, most ideal form, — first love as it should come once into the life of every human being.

Besides these two intense scenes, the one joyous, the other tragic, this novel is surcharged with aphorisms; it is a necklace of rich gems in which jewels of all kinds find place; sudden meteors of thought, comet-like flashes of wit, keen shafts of satire, and bursts of melodious rhetoric, compose the brilliant background of the novel; and against this, aided by it, the well-meaning but mistaken Bennet, the tender Lucy, the fair Lady Blandish, and the stormy Richard act out the dramas of their eventful lives. What a wonderful spectacle of life is " The Ordeal of Richard Feverel"! It is not only a work of genius, but a great moral tragedy; and it cannot fail to make an indelible impression upon the mind of every thoughtful reader.

It is only after we have exhausted the short walks in our neighborhood, where the paths are already cleared, that we attempt the more distant excursions, and cut our way through bush and bramble; so it is that, after we have enjoyed George Eliot's smooth English style, and Thackeray's simple conversational form of narrative, we shall feel tempted to break through the rough and tortuous sentences of George Meredith. But the effort once made, the rough pathway is soon forgotten, and we are amply repaid by the beauty of the landscape. The first steps demanded in overcoming the peculiar difficulties of Meredith's style require concentration and perseverance; but, these once taken, the reader becomes absorbed in the powerful and impressive soul-dramas which the great novelist creates and exhibits with such marvellous power.

"The Shaving of Shagpat," that strange web of Eastern fancies, was published in 1855, and was Meredith's first prose work. Next came "The Ordeal of Richard Feverel," in 1859, and in 1861 appeared "Evan Harrington." The contrast between "The Ordeal of Richard Feverel" and "Evan Harrington" is marked. For the first novel is a tragedy, and stirs our deepest and saddest emotions; the second novel is a comedy, and amuses us by making the antics of the human animals seem outrageously comic and absurd. "Evan Harrington" is devoted to portraying the vices and follies of fashionable life, and the particularly amusing vicissitudes of the Harrington family. The hero of the book, Evan, was the son of "Old Mel," a fashionable tailor; and the efforts made by his sister, the Portuguese Countess de Saldas, to conceal her father's profession, and to assist her brother to make a good marriage, are described with delicious humour. The character of the scheming Countess is drawn with immense skill, and even suggests that queen of adventuresses, Becky Sharp; but "Vanity Fair" is a satire, while "Evan Harrington" is an extravaganza; in the one novel real people walk and talk much as they do in life; in the other, the characters are all exaggerated, painted in broad scenic colors; they

need to be looked at from a distance, and do not bear
comparison with real personages. The men and
women in "Evan Harrington" talk in aphorisms,
and have metaphors at their tongue's end. They
weary us by their perpetual vivacity, and their strained,
inflated style of talking becomes after a time insuffer-
ably tedious. Unconsciously, Meredith permits his
own extraordinary wit and brilliancy to shine through
all his creations, forgetting that the habit of convers-
ing in epigrams is rare in common life. There is an
extraordinary amount of irrelevant matter in this
novel; and irrelevant matter, as a sharp critic says,
never lengthens, but buries a story. Meredith often
amuses himself by attempting a long series of mental
gymnastics; he starts some idle topic of conversation,
and then follows it on through endless ramifications
until it and the reader are completely exhausted; his
own mind is so synthetic, that it cannot help adding
to anything he takes into it. But there is some vigorous character-drawing in "Evan Harrington"; and
the writer makes the most of the contrast between
the complex, wire-pulling, deceitful, but fascinating
Countess, and the wholesome, clear-souled young
English girl, Rose Jocelyn, who is described as being,
at one moment, "the halcyon, and at another the
stormy petrel," but is always ingenuous and admirable. In the love-scene between Evan and Rose, the
tender poetic vein in Meredith's nature is again apparent: "Holy to them grew the stillness; the ripple
suffused in golden moonlight; the dark edges of the

leaves against superlative brightness. Not a chirp was heard, nor anything save the cool and endless carols of the happy waters, whose voices are the spirits of silence. Nature seems consenting that their hands should be joined, their eyes intermingling." This making an harmonious background out of nature, and using it to give an atmospheric quality to a love-scene, Meredith understands better than any modern writer except Turguenieff; many of Meredith's love-scenes are prose idyls; they are Tennysonian in their pastoral sweetness.

Following "Evan Harrington," in 1864, appeared "Emilia in England," and in 1865 "Rhoda Fleming." We prefer to consider "Rhoda Fleming" before we do "Emilia in England," published now under the name of "Sandra Belloni," because this last belongs with "Vittoria," the two being in purpose halves of one novel, though published separately.

In "Rhoda Fleming," Meredith turns away from fashionable society, and devotes himself to a study of life among the sturdy men and women of Kent. The virtues of courage, pride, and constancy, which are displayed by the hard-working country folk, are especially emphasized in this story. Rhoda Fleming, the heroine of the novel, with her strong, proud nature, and her indomitable will, is a new type of woman, in fiction; all her faults arise from her strength of character, and her over-confidence in her own judgment. She has a grand contempt for weakness and a holy scorn for sin. Her passionate, romantic love for her sister, and her mistaken belief in that sister's purity, give as pathetic a situation as any to be found in modern fiction. Edward Biancove, also, is a well-conceived character, — one of the complex, many-sided natures our involved modern civilization tends to produce; notwithstanding his delicate sensibilities and strong human feelings, he is unable to accept the responsibility of his acts, and goes through life, shirking consequences; this fatal lack of courage and tendency towards sentimentalism lead him to commit infamous deeds and cause endless suffering. The flimsy, fascinating Mrs. Lovell is another interesting study. What a contrast between her character and that of the devoted Dahlia! The one is all sincerity and heart; the other is scheming, secretive, and enigmatical.

Two more remarkable life-studies occur to us as we think over "Rhoda Fleming," — the spendthrift Algy and the miser Anthony; both these are wholly original conceptions; but what a grim, sad lesson this novel teaches! How pitilessly and unflinchingly does the writer make us face the consequences of sin! How full of tragic possibilities does life seem as we close its covers! Dahlia Fleming's fall and Edward Biancove's sin are facts which occur very frequently in fiction, and constantly in life; and Meredith has not let one thread in the awful web of consequences escape him; the fall of the proud, loving Dahlia, and the shame it brought upon her home, is so painful, so vividly described, that the reader who seeks merely for entertainment from a novel had best not open the covers of "Rhoda Fleming."

Before taking up "Vittoria" and "Sandra Belloni" we must mention the fact that George Meredith served as correspondent to the London Morning Post during the last Austro-Italian war in 1866, when Italy obtained her liberty. He did not go forward with the army, or see much actual fighting, but at Venice he had opportunities of studying the character and situations of the opposed forces; and the result of this study he gave to the world in "Vittoria," which was written at that time. This book is a series of strong, vivid impressions, full of color; but it is unpruned and overloaded with material. Its effect upon the reader is like the effect aroused by some great battle-scene on canvas; the artist's perseverance and courage in attempting such a colossal piece of work cause us to admire him, but we soon tire of gazing at the results of his Titanic efforts.

"Sandra Belloni" and "Vittoria" together form one extended recital, and make an exceedingly complicated organism, which is not easily taken apart; we doubt if any reader ever pushed his way through both of them without moments of fatigue. In these two volumes the writer follows the fortunes of one woman, who is a grandly conceived and finely drawn study. This woman — Emilia in England, afterwards Vittoria in Italy — was the daughter of an uneducated Italian living in England; she was born with a passion for music, and gifted with a wonderful voice; her musical talent led her to be invited to the house of a vulgar English family by the name of Pole. They are described by the writer as "perpetually mounting." One of this family, Wilfrid Pole, made love to Emilia, but soon gave her up because he dared not risk his social position by marrying a woman who had neither fortune nor family. The sisters of Wilfrid Pole are admirable pen-and-ink sketches; they supposed they enjoyed "exclusive possession of the nice feelings and fine shades." After Emilia discovered her lover's inconstancy she left England to devote herself to music and Italy; under the name of Vittoria she appears again in the second part, acting as leader in an Italian political conspiracy; in the guise of a *débutante* at the opera, she gives the signal for revolt by singing a solo with the patriotic refrain "Italia shall be free." This scene, the opening scene in "Vittoria," is a grandly dramatic one; it is the natural climax of the narrative, and the reader is sadly disappointed to find that the succeeding events do not grow increasingly interesting; the plot thickens only to grow more involved; the new threads which are introduced are crossed and tangled, and the reader grows desperate in attempting to disentangle the final snarl. In the midst of all this confusion stands out one grand, harmonious conception,—the character of Emilia; she is a heroine in every act of her life, perfectly equal to each emergency, thrilling with feeling, and yet controlling her emotion when occasion demands it for the good of others. She performs startling feats of heroism, but the greatest is her supreme mastery over herself. Still, with all these high qualities, there is some slight want in Emilia's nature; she is admirable, but not lovable; she is wonderful, but not winning. We do not open our hearts to her as we do to some of Meredith's more faulty creations. She is perhaps deficient in some subtle human quality, and stands like a beautiful statue far apart from life.

These two novels — "Sandra Belloni" and "Vittoria" — are striking proofs of the scope of Meredith's genius. He does not even confine himself to one national type, but has that breadth of insight which enables him to comprehend an alien race. His range of character is universal. In these two novels and in "The Adventures of Harry Richmond" the writer's style is less involved. We are puzzled and confused by fewer metaphors, and delighted by fewer epigrams. There is an apparent effort made by Meredith, at least in Vittoria and in Harry Richmond, to be more simple and more conventional. In "Emilia in England" the writer gives utterance to his own heretical literary creed: "The point to be considered is whether fiction demands a perfectly smooth surface. Undoubtedly a scientific work does, and a philosophic treatise should. When we ask for facts simply, we feel the intrusion of style. Of fiction it is a part. In the one case the classical robe, in the other any mediæval phantasy of clothing." Again, in this same novel he says: "A writer who is not servile, and has insight, must coin from his own mint. In prose we owe every-

thing to the license our poets have taken, in the teeth
of critics."
We will not linger with the colossal charlatan, in
Harry Richmond, save to say that immense imagi-
native power and a daring intellect were required
to conceive such a wildly sensational and absolutely improbable tale. In this book there are few
sententious sayings; all the author's energy went
towards preparing his extraordinary plot, and devel-
oping and arranging his great heterogeneous army
of characters.

"The Egoist," which followed "The Adventures of
Harry Richmond," is likewise stamped with Meredith's
most irritating peculiarities, and is more difficult for
a beginner to attack than any other of these novels.
It has a long Prelude, which can be read half a dozen
times without conveying any intelligible meaning to
the reader's mind; indeed, the writer calls it "a chapter of which the last page only is of any importance."
It is like a dark, tortuous, subterranean passage, into
which few rays of light penetrate, serving only to
make the darkness more palpable; whether the author
himself ever comes out anywhere, few of his readers
will be able to determine. The first part of "The
Egoist" must be taken on faith, — a faith grounded
on a knowledge of Meredith's power, gained from
reading "The Ordeal of Richard Feverel" and
"Beauchamp's Career"; but when once interest in
the fine analysis of Sir Willoughby Pattern's character is aroused, the book will be appreciated.

Stevenson has taken "The Egoist" into the circle of his intimates, and has read it four or five times. One English critic thinks it the most witty of all Meredith's novels; but an American critic, George Parsons Lathrop, calls it "an inflated, obese, elephantine comedy, which is not comic." Granted that it is inflated, obese, extravagant, and coarse, acknowledging all these faults, we yet claim that it is deliciously, spontaneously, and irresistibly humorous. Sir Willoughby is a type of incarnate selfishness and conceit. Perhaps no real person ever existed who was exactly his prototype, for he combines in his personality all possible phases of egotism. The consummate literary skill of Meredith is displayed in the development of this one thoroughly consistent character: Sir Willoughby is great in the way that many of Balzac's creations are great, — as a living, breathing embodiment of one strong characteristic; and every other personage in this novel is subservient to the Egoist. There are, however, other excellent character sketches, such as Mrs. Mountstuart Jenkinson, who "was a lady certain to say the remembered, if not the right thing," and had "her decided preference of persons that shone in the sun." There, too, is that beguiling young woman, Clara Middleton! We quote the description of her: "She was too beautiful. Whatever she did was best. That was the refrain of the fountain-song in him: the burden being her whims, variations, inconsistencies, wiles; her tremblings between good and naughty, that might be stamped to noble or to terrible; her sincereness, her duplicity, her courage, cowardice, possibilities for heroism or treachery. She was a creature of only naturally youthful wildness, provoked to freakishness by the ordeal of a situation shrewd as any that can happen to her sex in civilized life."

The blindly romantic Letitia Dale is another well-defined type in "The Egoist." In the contrast between the self-abnegating young girl longing to worship her ideal man, and the disappointed woman facing with open eyes her shattered idol, Meredith presents us with a great dramatic contrast. Letitia illustrates the pernicious consequences of a too blind worship of any one of God's creatures; her poor, bleeding heart is opened with a sharp dissecting-knife, and we are permitted to gaze upon it as its life-blood dries up, and it shrivels and withers away before our eyes. Where has Meredith obtained his knowledge of women's hearts? Nothing that is feminine is unknown to him; but what is to be said about the rough surface of "The Egoist"? How is the reader to overcome his dislike to the fantastic clothing under which the writer has chosen to conceal this great comedy? It can only be accepted as an inflexible characteristic of Meredith's manner, to be deplored, but endured. Just as a beautiful face may be injured by one bad feature, but not ruined, so, in considering a writer's merits, we must not let one prominent and aggressive fault deter us from appreciating what is truly admirable.

To the general reader, "Beauchamp's Career" will be more interesting than "The Egoist." It is crammed with incident, and the hero is the very antithesis of Sir Willoughby Pattern. Beauchamp was generous, idealistic, honourable, and passionately interested in the public weal. He was a man whose projects always failed, but whose failures call for more admiration than the most brilliant successes of others. He was a hero, and a hero-worshipper; yet his life was one long succession of mistakes. Beauchamp's character is by far the noblest and most lovable of all Meredith's masculine creations; he fought single-handed against the world, and fate and circumstances were too strong for him; but he stands out in our minds as the ideal youth, alive to all that is good, true, or beautiful in life. His only weakness lay in his excessive sensibility to the charms of woman. All women were adorable to him, and he adored more than his share of them. In this work we have a new gallery of feminine portraits; were there ever three more charming creations than Renée, Cecilia, and Jenny? Do we wonder that they all captivated the youthful Beauchamp? If we do, we must remember Meredith's sage remark, that "men open to passion have to be taught reflection before they distinguish between the woman they would sue for love because she would be their best mate, and the woman who has thrown a spell over them."

Dr. Shrapnel is one of the most striking personages in this novel. He is a rabid radical in politics, and a violent declaimer against the present social conditions in England. Perhaps in him the writer embodies many of his own political theories ; for Shrapnel is a mouthpiece rather than a personality ; he dogmatizes, philosophizes, and makes vigorous assaults upon the church, the clergy, the state, and the upper classes of society in Great Britain. Indeed, most of the aphorisms, of which there are two or three hundred in this novel, treat of political life. Dr. Shrapnel's philosophy, however, is not always either coherent or consistent. He strikes right and left, and hits at all existing forms of evil; but, like Carlyle, he contents himself with destroying and reviling, and rarely stops to rebuild. Beauchamp makes an idol of this great Radical, and follows him blindly ; and the younger man's capacity for hero-worship is a delightful feature in his many-sided character. Another delicately conceived relationship is the one which existed between Beauchamp and Rosamund. The pure yet absorbing love of an older woman for a brilliant, noble-minded boy has rarely been touched upon before by a novelist. The mixture of the maternal in Rosamund's feeling for Beauchamp is beautiful, and keeps the relationship from the least taint of sensuality or vulgarity ; in Beauchamp the lonely woman saw infinite possibilities, and her love for the divine in him was akin to the worship she lifted up to God.

The subtle psychic forces which unite individuals and decide their fates are studied scientifically in all Meredith's novels, but the working of these forces

is especially apparent in the book before us. In
Beauchamp's strong personal influence over all the
women he came in contact with, we see an illustration
of the magnetic power of moral beauty. His power of
attracting and holding love was almost magical.

Turning over the pages of "Beauchamp's Career" is
like looking into the glittering show-window of some
fashionable jeweller; the array of sparkling gems
dazzles us, but, to appreciate any one jewel, we must
detach it from its brilliant company, and let it shine
in solitary radiance. Every page of this novel is
crammed with aphorisms, but they so crowd one
another that no epigram has a chance of being esti-
mated at its full value. Besides the collection of rare
"seed-thoughts" and "gold-dust," which we find scattered so extravagantly through the pages of "Beauchamp's Career," the writer often delights us by
indulging himself in one of his tender lyrical moods.
Who, that has read this novel, is likely to forget the
glorious description of dawn upon the Adriatic? It
could only have dropped from the pen of a poet. It
recalls a familiar canto in "Childe Harold," and
tempts us to compare Meredith with the "noble poet";
for in spite of his contempt for the Byronic in life and
literature, — which Meredith translates to mean the
sentimental and insincere, — these two writers certainly had points in common; both were spontaneous,
and yet both were insensible, consciously or unconsciously, to artistic form. But while Byron was the
most subjective of poets, and never looked at the

world except through his own short-sighted eyes, Meredith has a wonderful faculty for getting outside himself, and for looking at life without reference to its effect upon his own individual career. That unhealthy feature of modern literature — the morbid introduction of the writer's personality into his novels, his poems, and even his essays — is a vice from which Meredith is absolutely free. He never consciously indulges himself in egoism. "Life immense in passion, pulse, and power," is so absorbingly interesting to him that he cannot afford to turn his back upon it and confine his attention within the narrow limits of his own Ego. The awe-inspiring spectacle of this manifold nineteenth century existence of ours presses upon Meredith as it does upon Walt Whitman. Our vision of life deepens and widens as we read these remarkable novels; and, forgetful of personal and petty woes, we turn with their author to face the facts of this universe with courage, hope, and reverence, desiring "to earn for the body and the mind whatever adheres and goes forward, and is not dropt by death."

The last prose publications of Meredith are "The Tragic Comedians" and "Diana of the Crossways." The former of these was published in the Fortnightly Review, in 1880 and 1881. It has never been republished in this country, and at the time it was written involved the writer unjustly in a serious charge of plagiarism. It is said to be the true story of Ferdinand Lassalle's life. It has more unity, and is condensed into a more compact form, than most of

Meredith's books; but here also the style is uncouth and the sentences are obscure and enigmatical. In "The Tragic Comedians" the writer gives much time and strength to moralizing and philosophizing, yet few of his reflections take form enough to be called aphorisms. His wit and wisdom in this story are like the delicate spring wild-flowers, beautiful amid their natural surrounding, but losing all strength and fragrance in the process of transplanting. The author's strange Preface to this book, in explanation of its eccentric title, is worth examination. Of his hero he writes: "He was neither fool nor madman, nor man to be adored; his last temptation caught him in the season before he had subdued his blood, and amid the multitudinously simple of the world stamped him as a tragic comedian; that is, a grand pretender, a self-deceiver, one of the lively ludicrous, whom we cannot laugh at, but must contemplate, to distinguish where their character strikes the note of discord with life; for otherwise, in the reflection of their history, life will seem a thing demoniacally inclined by fits to antic and dive into gulfs. The characters of the hosts of men are of the simple order of the comic; not many are of a stature and a complexity calling for the junction of the two Muses to name them." In this prolix passage Meredith is shown at his worst; he can spin out this sort of brain-stuff by the chapter, and has not enough literary tact to appreciate the fact that the public will not give ear to such vagaries, even though they be the vagaries of genius.

Last of all, we take up what has proved to be the most popular of all Meredith's novels. "Diana of the Crossways" is a story of the adventures and misadventures of a fashionable and witty society woman. The writer gives Diana beauty of body, brilliancy of mind, and all the lovable feminine qualities; she had an intellect which for keenness and versatility was far beyond the average masculine intellect. Wherever the perceptive power of the intellect led, she ruled supreme; but her "sense was with her senses all mixed up," and in every crisis of life she permitted herself to be ruled by her feelings. She relied for guidance chiefly upon her instincts, and not upon her reason, and had never disciplined her emotional nature to obey the dictates of hard common-sense. This fatal defect in the mental machinery of all women, Meredith sees and deplores. He never underestimates the capacity of the feminine mind; he delights in its playful antics, its delicate subtleties, and its quick sensitiveness to shades of thought and feeling; but the supreme faculty of reason, the highest, in Meredith's opinion, of all faculties, he finds as yet undeveloped in the weaker sex. The heart with them always "overrules the head"; their intellects, no matter how brilliant they may be, never forewarn them of danger, never control their actions in the crucial events of their lives. All the mistakes made by the fascinating Diana, in the book before us, are concrete illustrations of this theory. Women, according to Meredith's avowed theory, are volatile, inconsequent creatures, the slaves of every fleeting impulse; they may be clever in conversation, they may think deeply on abstract questions, but their lives are utterly inconsistent, and no one can ever tell what extraordinary, irrevocable mischief they may perpetrate at any moment. In Diana's betrayal of her lover's state secret, this theory is illustrated with great force; and not alone in this flagrant act, but in all Diana's life, do we see the writer's conception of "a woman's reason" disclosed. The cleverness of the "table-talk" in "Diana of the Crossways" is very remarkable; the conversations in this novel are worthy to be compared for brilliancy with any which took place in the *salons* of the Rambouillet before the society of the Précieuses degenerated and became ridiculous. There may be a difference of opinion about this book considered as a novel. It does not sufficiently conform to all the rules of art to be approved by critics of the highest standard; but there can be no divergence of taste as to the merits of its clever dialogues, and the wit of its many incisive idiomatic epigrams.

By close attention to the rules of narrative, to what Besant calls "the art of fiction," many a writer can produce novels which will have fewer faults in construction than George Meredith's; but there is a gift of the Gods, a *clairvoyance*, never attained by any amount of perseverance, which is the dower of great minds, among whom we must class George Meredith. Nothing is easier than to point out Meredith's faults. They force themselves upon us at every step we take within his literary territory. Nor are they subtle faults, which require a fine critical eye to discern them; they annoy us like the inevitable thorns on a moss-rose bud; they often bar our progress through his novels like the points on a barbed-wire fence. But why should we undertake the enumeration of these defects? It is a vain and ungrateful task; and the object of this little volume is to lead readers to pursue a totally different method of criticism. We have endeavoured to select from twelve volumes of prose and three of verse the best that Meredith has said and sung, for the purpose of gaining for him at least a sympathetic hearing. With this end in view, we have chosen and collected aphorisms long and short, witty epigrams, idiomatic phrases, and philosophical reflections upon life; and we have added a few exquisite lyrical prose passages, and several entire poems, making an effort to ignore the obscure and abstruse, and to present the public with only what will be intelligible and attractive at the first reading.

To those who already revere Meredith, and count his books among their familiar friends, this compilation will seem a needless task. They love him and his work too sincerely to be ever satisfied with fragmentary excerpts; but the compiler who gains new readers for a great writer, who opens up to any reader a new mine of intellectual treasure, is perhaps of some slight service to the literary world. It is to those, therefore, who have never dared to go beyond the incomprehensible Preface to "The Egoist," who

INTRODUCTION.

have been provoked to wrath by the first pages of "Diana of the Crossways," who have stumbled over the halting stanzas of "Grandfather Bridgeman," that this small volume of excerpts is dedicated.

Matthew Arnold tells us that the best tribute we can pay an author is, not to cover him with eloquent eulogy, but to let him, at his best and greatest, speak for himself; and it is in the hope of gaining for this great philosophical novelist such an opportunity, that these selections from his works have been made.

It is surely with a lofty conception of his high vocation, and with true humility, that the poet Meredith sings: —

> "Assured of worthiness, we do not dread
> Competitors; we rather give them hail
> And greeting in the lists where we may fail;
> Must if we bear an aim beyond the head!
> My betters are my masters; purely fed,
> By their sustainment I likewise shall scale
> Some rocky steps between the mount and vale:
> Meantime the mark I have and I will wed,
> So that I draw the breath of finer air,
> Station is naught, nor footways laurel-strewn,
> My rivals tightly belted for the race
> Good speed to them! My place is here or there;
> My pride is that among them I have place;
> And thus I keep this instrument in tune."

M R. F. GILMAN.

CONCORD, N. H., *September* 1, 1888.

THE
ORDEAL OF RICHARD FEVEREL.

THE
ORDEAL OF RICHARD FEVEREL.

Love is the blessed wand which wins the waters from the hardness of the heart.

The born preacher we feel instinctively to be our foe. He may do some good to the wretches who have been struck down and lie gasping on the battle-field: he rouses antagonism in the strong.

If immeasurable love were perfect wisdom, one human being might almost impersonate Providence to another. Alas! love, divine as it is, can do no more than lighten the house it inhabits; must take its shape, sometimes intensify its narrowness; can spiritualize, but not expel, the old life-long lodgers above stairs and below.

CONSIDER the sort of minds influenced by set sayings. A proverb is the half-way house to an idea, I conceive, and the majority rest there content: can the keeper of such a house be flattered by his company?

WHERE is the fortress that has not one weak gate? Where the man who is sound at each particular angle? Ay, meditates the recumbent cynic, more or less mad is not every mother's son? Favorable circumstances, good air, good company, two or three rules rigidly adhered to, keep the world out of Bedlam. But let the world fly into a passion, and is not Bedlam the safest abode for it?

To talk nonsense or poetry, or the dash between the two, in a tone of profound sincerity, and to enunciate solemn discordances with received opinion so seriously as to convey the impression of a spiritual insight, is the peculiar gift by which monomaniacs, having first persuaded themselves, contrive to influence their neighbors, and through them make conquest of a good half of the world for good or for ill.

POETRY, love, and such-like are the drugs earth has to offer to high natures, as she offers to low ones debauchery.

WHEN Nature has made us ripe for love, it seldom occurs that the Fates are behindhand in furnishing a temple for the flame.

SIR AUSTIN and Mrs. Caroline discovered that they had in common from an early period looked on life as a science; and having arrived at this joint understanding, they, with the indifference of practised dissectors, laid out the world and applied the knife to the people they knew. In other words, they talked most frightful scandal.

BECAUSE the heavens are certainly propitious to true lovers, the beasts of the abysses are banded to destroy them, stimulated by innumerable sad victories; and every love-tale is an epic war of the upper and lower powers.

WITH the onward flow of intimacy the two happy lovers ceased to be so shy of common themes, and their speech did not reject all as dross that was not pure gold of emotion.

At their tryst in the wood abutting on Raynham Park, wrapped in themselves, piped to by tireless love, Richard and Lucy sat toying with eternal moments. How they seem as if they would never end! What mere sparks they are when they have died out! And how in the distance of time they revive and extend and glow, and make us think them full the half, and the best, of the fire of our lives!

To anchor the heart by any object ere we have half traversed the world, is youth's foolishness.

Love of any human object is the soul's ordeal.

There are ideas language is too gross for, and shape too arbitrary, which come to us and have a definite influence upon us; and yet we cannot fasten on the filmy things and make them visible and distinct to ourselves, much less to others.

Know you those wand-like touches of I know not what, before which our grosser being melts, and we, much as we hope to be in the Awakening, stand etherealized, trembling with new joy? They come but rarely,—rarely even in love, when we fondly think them revelations. Mere sensations they are, doubtless; and we can rank for them no higher in the spiritual scale than so many translucent glorious polypi that quiver on the shores, the hues of heaven running through them. Yet in the harvest of our days it is something for the animal to have had such mere fleshly polypian experiences to look back upon, and they give him an horizon, — pale seas of luring splendor.

"LET us remember," says the Pilgrim's Scrip, "that Nature, though heathenish, reaches at her best to the footstool of the Highest. She is not all dust, but a living portion of the spheres. In aspiration it is our error to despise her, forgetting that through Nature only can we ascend."

SENTIMENTALISTS are they who seek to enjoy without incurring the immense debtorship for a thing done.

A POOR dyspepsy may talk as he will, but he is the one who never gets sympathy, or experiences compassion; and it is he whose groaning petitions for charity do at last rout that Christian virtue.

Sir Austin had also small patience for his brother's gleam of health, which was just enough to make his disease visible.

They say that when the skill and care of men rescue a drowned wretch from extinction and warm the flickering spirit into steady flame, such pain it is, the blood forcing its way along the dry channels and the heavily ticking nerves and the sullen heart; the struggle of Life and Death in him; grim Death relaxing his gripe,—such pain it is, he cries out no thanks to them that pull him by inches from the depths of the dead river. And he who has thought a love extinct, and is surprised by the old fires and the old tyranny,—he rebels, and strives to fight clear of the cloud of forgotten sensations that settle on him; such pain it is, the old, sweet music reviving through his frame, and the charm of his passion fixing him afresh.

There is a power in their troubled beauty women learn the use of; and what wonder? They have seen it kindle Ilium to flames so often! But ere they grow matronly in the house of Menelaus they weep and implore, and do not in truth know how terribly two-edged is their gift of loveliness. Love the charioteer is easily tripped; while honest jog-trot Love keeps his legs to the end.

HER conduct drove Mrs. Berry from the rosy to the autumnal view of matrimony, — generally heralded by the announcement that it is a lottery.

ALTHOUGH it blew hard when Cæsar crossed the Rubicon, the passage of that river is commonly calm, — calm as Acheron. So long as he gets his fare, the ferryman does not need to be told whom he carries; he pulls with a will, and heroes may be over in half an hour. Only when they stand on the opposite bank do they see what a leap they have taken; the shores they have relinquished shrink to an infinite remoteness. There they have dreamed; here they must act. There lie youth and irresolution; here manhood and purpose. They are veritably in another land; a moral Acheron divides their life. Their memories scarce seem their own.

The "Philosophical Geography" about to be published observes that each man has, one time or other, a little Rubicon — a clear or a foul water — to cross. It is asked him, "Wilt thou wed this Fate, and give up all behind thee?" And "I will," firmly pronounced, speeds him over. The above-named manuscript authority informs us that by far the greater number of carcases rolled by this heroic flood to its sister stream below are those of fellows who have repented their pledge and have tried to swim back to the bank they have blotted out. For though every man of us may be a hero for one fatal minute, very few remain so after a day's march even; and who wonders that Madame Fate is indignant, and wears the features of the terrible universal Fate to him?

The danger of a little knowledge of things is disputable; but beware the little knowledge of one's self.

It is difficult for those who think very earnestly for their children to know when their children are thinking on their own account. The exercise of their volition we construe for revolt. Our love does not like to be invalided and deposed from its command; and here I think yonder old thrush on the lawn, who has just kicked the last of her lank offspring out of the nest to go shift for itself, much the kinder of the two, though sentimental people do shrug their shoulders at these unsentimental acts of the creatures who wander from Nature.

THE reason why men and women are mysterious to us, and prove disappointing, is that we will read them from our own book, just as we are perplexed by reading ourselves from theirs.

EACH woman is Eve throughout the ages; whereas the Pilgrim would have us believe that the Adam in men has become warier, if not wiser, and, weak as he is, has learned a lesson from time. Probably the Pilgrim's meaning may be taken to be that man grows, and woman does not.

THE Pilgrim may be wrong about the sex not growing; but its fashion of conducting warfare we must allow to be barbarous, and according to what is deemed the pristine, or wildcat, method.

When a soft woman, and that soft woman a sinner, is matched with a woman of energy, she does not show much fight, and she meets no mercy.

The honeymoon was shining placidly above them. Is not happiness like another circulating medium? When we have a very great deal of it, some poor hearts are aching for what is taken away from them. When we have gone out and seized it on the highways, certain inscrutable laws are sure to be at work to bring us to the criminal bar sooner or later. Who knows the honeymoon that did not steal somebody's sweetness?

The God of this world is in the machine, not out of it.

How are we to know when we are at the head and fountain of the fates of them we love?

There are hours when the clearest soul becomes a cunning fox.

Sir Austin had a weak digestion for wrath. Instead of eating it, it ate him. The wild beast was not the less deadly because it did not roar, and the devil in him not the less active because he resolved to do nothing.

From that moment she grew critical of him, and began to study her idol, — a process dangerous to idols.

Speech is the small change of silence.

The honeymoon is Mahomet's minute, — or say the Persian king's water-pail that you read of in the story. You dip your head in it, and when you draw it out you discover you have lived a life.

The small debate in the baronet's mind ended by his throwing the burden on Time, — Time would bring the matter about. Christians as well as pagans are in the habit of phrasing this excuse for folding their arms, forgetful that the Devil's imps enter into no such armistice.

THE language of the two social extremes is similar. I find it to consist in an instinctively lavish use of vowels and adjectives. My Lord and Farmer Blaize speak the same tongue, only my Lord's has lost its backbone, and is limp, though fluent. Their pursuits are identical, but that one has money, or, as the Pilgrim terms it, *vantage*, and the other has not. Their ideas seem to have a special relationship in the peculiarity of stopping where they have begun. . . . This sounds dreadfully democratic. Pray don't be alarmed. The discovery of the affinity between the two extremes of the Royal British Oak has made me thrice Conservative. I see now that the national love of a lord is less subservience than a form of self-love, — putting a gold-lace hat on one's image, as it were, to bow to it. I see, too, the admirable wisdom of our system : could there be a finer balance of power than in a community where men intellectually *nil* have lawful vantage and a gold-lace hat on? How soothing it is to intellect — that noble rebel, as the Pilgrim has it — to stand and bow and know itself superior ! This exquisite compensation maintains the balance ; whereas that period anticipated by the Pilgrim, when science shall have produced an intellectual aristocracy, is indeed horrible to contemplate. For what despotism is so black as one the mind cannot challenge?

BUT to be passive in calamity is the province of no woman. Mark the race at any hour. What revolution and hubbub does not that little instrument, the needle, avert from us!

YOUNG men take joy in nothing so much as the thinking women angels; and nothing sours men of experience more than knowing that all are not quite so.

HIS indigestion of wrath had made of him a moral dyspepsy.

"LAUGH away," said Mrs. Berry; "I don't mind ye. I say again, we all do know what checked prespiration is. It fly to the lungs, it gives ye mortal inflammation, and it carries ye off. Then I say checked matrimony is as bad. It fly to the heart, and it carries off the virtue that's in ye, and you might as well be dead! Them that is joined, it's their salvation not to separate! It don't so much matter before it. That Mr. Thompson there, — if he go astray it ain't from the blessed fold. He hurt himself alone. . . . I'm for holding back young people so that they knows their minds, howsomever they rattles about their hearts. I ain't a speeder of matrimony, and good's my reason! But where it's been done, where they're lawfully joined and their bodies made one, I do say this: that to put division between 'em then, it's to make wanderin' comets of 'em, — creatures without a objeck; and no soul can say what they's good for but to rush about!"

IN love, Mrs. Berry's charity was all on the side of the law, — and this is the case with many of her sisters.

SHE could read men with one quiver of her half-closed eyelashes. She could catch the coming mood of a man and fit herself to it. What does a woman want with ideas who can do this? Keenness of perception, conformity, delicacy of handling, these be all the qualities necessary to parasites. . . . Various as the serpent of old Nile, she acted fallen beauty, humorous indifference, reckless daring, arrogance in ruin.

WHAT she liked him for, she rather (very slightly) wished to do away with, or see if it could be done away with, — just as one wishes to catch a pretty butterfly without hurting its patterned wings. No harm intended to the innocent insect, only one wants to inspect it thoroughly and enjoy the marvel of it, in one's tender possession, and have the felicity of thinking one could crush it if one would.

HEROES, however, are not in the habit of wording their declarations of war at all. Lance in rest, they challenge and they charge. Like women, they trust to instinct, and graft on it the muscle of men. Wide fly the leisurely remonstrating hosts; institutions are scattered, they know not wherefore; heads are broken that have not the balm of a reason why. 'T is instinct strikes. Surely there is something divine in instinct!

SHE told him stories of blooming dames of good repute, and poured a little social sewerage into his ears.

THERE is something impressive in a great human hulk writhing under the unutterable torments of a mastery he cannot contend with, or account for, or explain by means of intelligible words.

THE heroine, in common with the hero, has her ambition to be of use in the world, — to do some good; and the task of reclaiming a bad man is extremely seductive to good women. Dear to their tender hearts as old china is a bad man they are mending.

THE Aphorist read himself so well that to juggle with himself was a necessity. As he wished the world to see him, he beheld himself: one who entirely put aside mere personal feelings; one in whom parental duty, based on the science of life, was paramount, — a scientific humanist, in short.

HIS was an order of mind that would accept the most burdensome charges, and by some species of moral usury make a profit out of them.

"ONE gets so addle-pated thinkin' many things," said Mrs. Berry, simply; "that's why we see won-

der clever people al'ays goin' wrong — to my mind.
I think it's al'ays the plan in a dielemmer to
pray God and walk forward."

"BELIEVIN' our idees o' matrimony to be sim'lar,
then I'll say, once married, married for life! Yes!
I don't even like widows. For I can't stop at
the grave, not at the tomb I can't stop. My
husband's my husband, and if I'm a body at the
resurrection, I say, speaking humbly, my Berry is
the husband o' my body; and to think of two
claimin' of me, — it makes me hot all over! Such
is my notion of that state between man and
woman. No givin' in marriage o' course, I know,
and if so, I'm single."

RICHARD is face to face with death for the first
time. He sees the sculpture of clay, — the spark
is gone.

CHARACTER! he has the character of a bullet
with a treble charge of powder behind it. Enthusiasm is the powder. That boy could get up an
enthusiasm for the maiden days of Ops.

Sentimental people are sure to live long and die fat. 'T is feeling that 's the slayer. Sentiment! 't is the cajolery of existence, the soft bloom which whoso weareth, he or she is enviable.

"He 's off in his heroics," said Mrs. Berry; "he want to be doin' all sorts of things: I say he 'll never do anything grander than that baby."

The phantasmic groupings of the young brain are very like those we see in the skies, and equally the sport of the wind.

Nonsense of enthusiasts is very different from nonsense of ninnies.

A maker of proverbs, — what is he but a narrow mind, the mouthpiece of narrower?

Which is the coward among us? He who sneers at the failings of humanity.

The autumn-primrose blooms for the loftiest manhood; is a vindictive flower in lesser hands.

Beauty of course is for the hero. Nevertheless, it is not always he on whom Beauty works its most conquering influence. It is the dull, commonplace man, into whose slow brain she drops like a celestial light, and burns lastingly. The poet, for instance, is a connoisseur of Beauty; to the artist she is the model. These gentlemen, by much contemplation of her charms, wax critical. The days when they had hearts being gone, they are haply divided between the blonde and the brunette; the aquiline nose and the Proserpine; this shaped eye and that. But go about among simple, unprofessional fellows, boors, dunderheads, and here and there you shall find some barbarous intelligence which has had just strength enough to conceive and has taken Beauty as its goddess, and knows but one form to worship in its poor, stupid fashion, and would perish for her. Nay, more, the man would devote all his day to her, though he is dumb as a dog. And, indeed, he is Beauty's dog. Almost every Beauty has her dog. The hero possesses her; the poet proclaims her; the painter puts her upon canvas; and the faithful old dog follows her; and the end of it is that the faithful old dog is her single attendant. Sir Hero is revelling in the wars or in Armida's bowers; Mr. Poet has spied a wrinkle; the brush is for the rose in its season. She turns to her old dog then; she hugs him; and he who has subsisted on a bone and a pat till there he squats decrepid, he turns his grateful old eye up to her, and has not a notion she is hugging sad memories in him, Hero, Poet, Painter, in one scrubby one! Then is she buried, and the village hears languid howls, and there is a paragraph in the newspapers concerning the extraordinary fidelity of an old dog.

LET it be some apology for the damage caused by the careering hero, and a consolation to the quiet wretches dragged along with him at his chariot-wheels, that he is generally the last to know when he has made an actual start,— such a mere creature is he, like the rest of us, albeit the head of our fates. By this you perceive the true hero, whether he be a prince or a pot-boy, that he does not plot; Fortune does all for him. He may be compared to one to whom, in an electric circle, it is given to carry the battery. We

caper and grimace at his will; yet not his the
will, not his the power. 'T is all Fortune's, whose
puppet he is. She deals her dispensations through
him. Yea, though our capers be never so comical,
he laughs not. Intent upon his own business, the
true hero asks little services of us here and there ;
thinks it quite natural they should be acceded to,
and sees nothing ridiculous in the lamentable contortions we must go through to fulfil them. Probably he is the elect of Fortune because of that
notable faculty of being intent on his own business.

THERE was no middle course for Richard's com-
rades between high friendship and absolute slavery. He was deficient in those cosmopolite habits
and feelings which enable boys and men to hold
together without caring much for each other; and,
like every insulated mortal, he attributed the defi-
ciency, of which he was quite aware, to the fact of
possessing a superior nature.

THERE is no more grievous sight, as there is no
greater perversion, than a wise man at the mercy of
his feelings.

EVAN HARRINGTON.

EVAN HARRINGTON.

A YOUTH who is engaged in the occupation of eating his heart, cannot shine to advantage, and is as much a burden to himself as he is an enigma to others.

SPEECH that has to be hauled from the depths usually betrays the effort.

MOST youths are like Pope's women, — they have no character at all. And indeed a character that does not wait for circumstances to shape it, is of small worth in the race that must be run. To be set too early, is to take the work out of the hands of the Sculptor who fashions men.

PRIDE was the one developed faculty of Evan's nature. The Fates who mould us always work from the mainspring.

We are now and then above our own actions, — seldom on a level with them.

Money is the clothing of a gentleman; he may wear it well or ill. Some, you will mark, carry great quantities of it gracefully; some, with a stinted supply, present a decent appearance; very few, I imagine, will bear inspection who are absolutely stripped of it.

Rare as epic song is the man who is thorough in what he does. And happily so; for in life he subjugates us, and he makes us bondsmen to his ashes.

A purpose wedded to plans may easily suffer shipwreck; but an unfettered purpose, that moulds circumstances as they rise, masters us, and is terrible. Character melts to it, like metal in the steady furnace.

The projector of plots is but a miserable gambler and votary of chances. Of a far higher quality is the will that can subdue itself to wait, and lay no petty traps for opportunity.

THERE is that in the aspect of a fine frame breathing hard facts which, to a youth who has been tumbled headlong from his card-castles and airy fabrics, is masterful, and like the pressure of a Fate.

WOMEN, who are almost as deeply bound to habit as old gentlemen, possess more of its spiritual element, and are warned by dreams, omens, creepings of the flesh, unwonted chills, suicide of china, and other shadowing signs, when a break is to be anticipated or has occurred.

A MERCURIAL temperament makes quicksilver of any amount of cash.

A MISERY beyond our own is a wholesome picture for youth; and though we may not for the moment compare the deep with the lower deep, we, if we have a heart for outer sorrows, can forget ourselves in it.

BOTH Ale and Eve seem to speak imperiously to the soul of man. See that they be good, see that they come in season, and we bow to the consequences.

There is danger, when you are forcing a merry countenance before the mirror presented to you by your kind, that your features, unless severely practised, will enlarge beyond the artistic limits, and degenerate to a grimace.

We mortals, the best of us, may be silly sheep in our likes and dislikes: where there is no premeditated or instinctive antagonism, we can be led into warm acknowledgment of merits we have not sounded.

We return to our first ambitions as to our first loves; not that they are dearer to us, — quit that delusion; our ripened loves and mature ambitions are probably closest to our hearts, as they deserve to be: but we return to them because our youth has a hold on us which it asserts whenever a disappointment knocks us down. Our old loves are always lurking to avenge themselves on the new by tempting us to a little retrograde infidelity.

Note that in all material fashions, as in all moral observances, women demand a circumference, and enlarge it more and more as civilization advances. Respect the mighty instinct, however mysterious it seem.

OUR comedies are frequently youth's tragedies.

LET a girl talk with her own heart an hour, and she is almost a woman.

TOUCHING a nerve is one of those unforgivable small offences which in our civilized state produce the social vendettas and dramas that, with savage nations, spring from the spilling of blood. Instead of an eye for an eye, a tooth for a tooth, we demand a nerve for a nerve. "Thou hast touched me where I am tender: thee too will I touch."

EVERY dinner may be said to have its special topic, just as every age has its marked reputation. They are put up twice or thrice, and have to contend with minor lights and to swallow them; and then they command the tongues of men, and flow uninterruptedly.

LOVE may spring in the bosom of a young girl like Hesper in the evening sky,— a gray speck in a field of gray, and not to be seen or known; till surely, as the circle advances, the faint planet gathers fire, and, coming nearer earth, dilates, and will and must be seen and known.

There is mob-rule in minds as in communities.

Mrs. Melville was a specimen of the arrant British wife, — inflexible in her own virtue, and never certain of her husband's when he was out of sight; a noble being, but somewhat wanting in confidence and Christianity.

That small motives are at the bottom of many illustrious actions, is a modern discovery.

Now the sense of honour, and of the necessity of acting the part it imposes on him, may be very strong in a young man; but certainly the sense of ridicule is more poignant.

It is no insignificant contest when love has to crush self-love utterly. At moments it can be done. Love has divine moments. There are times also when Love draws part of his being from self-love, and can find no support without it.

If it be a distinct point of wisdom to hug the hour that is, then does dinner amount to a highly intellectual invitation to man, for it furnishes the occasion; and Britons are the wisest of their race, for more than all others they take advantage of it. In this, Nature is undoubtedly our guide, seeing that he who, while feasting his body, allows to his soul a thought for the morrow, is in his digestion cursed, and becomes a house of evil humors. Now, though the epicure may complain of the cold meats, a dazzling table, a buzzing company, blue sky, and a band of music are incentives to the forgetfulness of troubles past and imminent, and produce a concentration of the faculties.

In this struggle with society I see one of the instances where success is entirely to be honoured, and remains a proof of merit. For however boldly antagonism may storm the ranks of society, it will certainly be repelled, whereas affinity cannot be resisted; and they who, against obstacles of birth, claim and keep their position among the educated and refined have that affinity.

Do not despise a virtue purely Pagan! The young who can act readily up to the Christian light are happier, doubtless, but they are led, they are passive; I think they do not make such capital Christians subsequently. They are never in such danger, we know; but some in the flock are more than sheep. The heathen ideal it is not so very easy to attain; and those who mount from it to the Christian have, in my humble thought, a firmer footing.

WHEN love is hurt, it is self-love that requires the opiate.

AFTER a big blow, a very little one scarcely counts. What are outward forms and social ignominies to him whose heart has been struck to the dust?

IT is false to imagine that schemers and workers in the dark are destitute of the saving gift of conscience. They have it, and it is perhaps made livelier in them than with easy people ; and therefore they are imperatively spurred to hoodwink it. Hence their self-delusion is deep, and endures. They march to their object, and, gaining or losing it, the voice that calls to them is the voice of a blind creature, whom any answer, provided the answer is ready, will satisfy. . . . When finally they snatch their minute of sight on the threshold of black night, their souls may compare with yonder shining circle on the ceiling, which, as the night-light below gasps for air, contracts, and extends but to mingle with the darkness. They would be nobler, better, boundlessly good to all,— to those whom they have injured. Alas ! for any definite deed, the limit of their circle is immovable, and they must act within it. The trick they have played themselves imprisons them.

SANDRA BELLONI.

SANDRA BELLONI.

It is still a good way from the head of the tallest man to the stars.

SENTIMENTALISTS are a perfectly natural growth of a fat soil. Wealthy communities must engender them. If with attentive minds we mark the origin of classes, we shall discern that the *nice feelings* and the *fine shades* play a principal part in our human development and social history. I dare not say that civilized man is to be studied with the eye of a naturalist; but my vulgar meaning might almost be twisted to convey that our sentimentalists are a variety owing their existence to a certain prolonged term of comfortable feeling. The pig, it will be retorted, passes likewise through this training. He does. But in him it is not combined with an indigestion of High-German romances.

Here is so notable a difference that he cannot possibly be said to be of the family. And I maintain it against him, who have nevertheless listened attentively to the eulogies pronounced by the venders of prize bacon.

WOMEN cannot repose on a man who is not positive; nor have they much gratification in confounding him. Wouldst thou, O man amorously inclining, attract to thee superior women, be positive, be stupidly positive, rather than dubious at all. Face fearful questions with a visor of brass. Array thyself in dogmas. Show thy decisive judgment on the side of established power, or thy enthusiasm in the rebel ranks, if it must be so; but be firm. Waver not. If women could tolerate waverings and weakness, and did not rush to the adoration of decision of mind, we should not behold them turning contemptuously from philosophers in their agony to take refuge in smirking orthodoxy.

THE parasite completes the animal, and a dependant assures us of our position.

The philosopher bids us mark that the crown and flower of the nervous system, the head, is necessarily sensitive, and to that degree that whatsoever we place on it does for a certain period change and shape us. Of course the instant we call up the forces of the brain much of the impression departs; but what remains is powerful and fine-nerved. Woman is especially subject to it. A girl may put on her brother's boots, and they will not affect her spirit strongly; but as soon as she puts on her brother's hat, she gives him a manly nod. The same philosopher, who fathers his dulness on me, asserts that the modern vice of fastness (trotting on " the Epicene Border " he has it) is bred by apparently harmless practices of this description. He offers to turn the current of a republican's brain by resting a coronet on his forehead for just five seconds.

———

When the youth is called upon to look up, he can adore devoutly and ardently; but when it is his chance to look down on a fair head, he is, if not worse, a sentimental despot.

SELECTION can only be made from a crowd. It is where we see few that we are at the mercy of kind fortune for our acquaintances.

WHEN we say we know any one, we mean commonly that we are accustomed to his ways and habits of mind, or that we can reckon on the predominant influences of his appetites. Sometimes we can tell which impulse is likely to be the most active, and which principle the least restraining. The only knowledge to be trusted is a grounded, or scientific study of the springs that move him, side by side with his method of moving the springs.

HIGHLY civilized natures do sometimes, and keen wits must always, feel dissatisfied when they are not on the laughing side; their dread of laughter is an instinctive respect for it.

No ridicule knocks the strength out of us so thoroughly as our own.

JUST as children will pinch themselves, pleased, up to the verge of unendurable pain, so do sentimentalists find a keen relish in performing *secret penance* for self-accused offences. Thus they become righteous to their own hearts, and evade, as they hope, the public scourge.

LITTLE people think either what they are made to think, or what they choose to think; and the education of girls is to make them believe that facts are their enemies.

SHE [Cornelia] affected in her restlessness to think that her spirits required an intellectual sedative; so she went to the library for a book, where she skimmed many, — a fashion that may be recommended for assisting us to a sense of sovereign superiority to authors, and also of serene contempt for all mental difficulties.

A HAPPY audacity of expression may pass. It is bad taste to repeat it.

IN love we have some idea whither we would go; in harness we are simply driven, and the destination may be anywhere.

All of us are weak in the period of growth, and are of small worth before the hour of trial. This fellow had been fattening all his life on prosperity, — the very best dish in the world; but it does not prove us. Adversity is the inspector of our constitutions; she simply tries our muscle and powers of endurance, and should be a periodical visitor. But until she comes, no man is known.

Man is the laughing animal; and at the end of an infinite search, the philosopher finds himself clinging to laughter as the best of human fruit,— purely human and sane and comforting. So let us be cordially thankful to those who furnish matter for sound embracing laughter.

The man who speculates blindfold is a fowl who walks into market to be plucked.

Can you pray? Can you put away all props of self? This is true worship, unto whatsoever Power you kneel.

The two men composing most of us at the outset of actual life began their deadly wrestle within him, both having become awakened. If they wait for circumstance, that steady fire will fuse them into one, who is commonly a person of some strength; but throttling is the custom between them, and we are used to see men of murdered halves. These men have what they fought for; they are unaware of any guilt that may be charged against them, though they know that they do not embrace Life; and so it is that we have vague discontent too universal. Change, O Lawgiver! the length of our minority, and let it not end till this battle is thoroughly fought out in approving daylight. The period of our duality should be one as irresponsible in your eyes as that of our infancy. Is he we call a young man an individual, who is a pair of alternately kicking scales? He has drunk Latin like a vital air, and can quote what he remembers of Homer; but how has he been fortified for this tremendous conflict of opening manhood, which is to our life here what is the landing of a soul to the life to come?

DISAPPOINTMENT vitiated many of Lady Charlotte's first impulses; and not until strong antagonism had thrown her upon her generosity could she do justice to the finer natures about her. There was full life in her veins, and she was hearing the thirty fatal bells that should be music to a woman, if melancholy music; and she had not lived. Time, that sounded in her ears, as it kindled no past, spoke of no future. She was in unceasing rivalry with all of her sex who had a passion, or a fixed affection, or even an employment. A sense that she was wronged by her fate, haunted this lady. Rivalry on behalf of a man she would have held mean, she would have plucked it from her bosom at once. She was simply envious of those who in the face of death could say, "I have lived." Pride and the absence of self-inspection kept her blind to her disease. No recollection gave her joy, save of the hours in the hunting-field. There she led gallantly; but it was not because of leading that she exulted. There the quick blood struck on her brain like wine, and she seemed for the time to have one of the crowns of life. An object — who cared how small? — was ahead: a poor fox trying to save his brush; and Charlotte would have it if the master of cunning did not beat her. "It's my natural thirst for blood," she said. She did not laugh now and then that the old red brush dragging over gray dews towards a yellow *yolk* in the curdled winter morning sky was the single thing that could make her heart throb.

THE truth is, we rarely indulge in melancholy until we take it as a luxury.

DESPAIR, as I have said before, is a wilful business, common to corrupt blood, and to weak, woful minds; native to the sentimentalist of the better order.

THE submerged self — self in the depths — rarely speaks to the occasion, but lies under the calamity, quietly apprehending all, willing that the talker overhead (the surface self) should deceive others, and herself likewise, if possible.

MALICE is the barb of beauty.

PASSION is noble strength on fire.

THE reproaching of Providence by a man of full growth comes to some extent from his meanness, and chiefly from his pride. He remembers that the old gods selected great heroes whom to persecute, and it is his compensation for material losses to conceive himself a distinguished mark for the powers of air. One who wraps himself in this delusion may have great qualities; he cannot be of a very contemptible nature; and in this place we will discriminate more closely than to call him a fool.

RHODA FLEMING.

RHODA FLEMING.

Our deathlessness is in what we do, not in what we are. . . . Young men easily fancy that when the black volume is shut, the tide is stopped. Saying "I was a fool," they believe they have put an end to the foolishness. What father teaches them that a human act, once set in motion, flows on forever to the great account?

The characteristic of girls having a disposition to rise is to be cravingly mimetic.

There is a fate attached to some women, from Helen of Troy downward, that blood is to be shed for them.

The day indeed is sad when we see the skeleton of the mistress by whom we suffer, but cannot abandon her.

THE office of critic is now, in fact, virtually extinct; the taste for tickling and slapping is universal and imperative. Classic appeals to the intellect, and passions not purely domestic, have grown obsolete.

COUNTRY people are not inclined to tolerate the display of a passion for anything. They find it as intrusive and exasperating as is, in the midst of larger congregations, what we call genius.

VETERANS in their arm-chairs strip the bloom from life, and show it to be bare bones. They take their wisdom for an experience of the past; they are but giving their sensations in the present. Not to perceive this is youth's error when it hears old gentlemen talking at their ease.

MAN'S aim is to culminate; but it is the saddest thing in the world to feel that we have accomplished it.

WHEN we appear most incongruous, we are often exposing the key to our characters.

Women can make for themselves new spheres, new laws, if they will assume their right to be eccentric as an unquestionable thing, and always reserve a season for showing forth, like the conventional women of society.

Silence is commonly the slow poison used by those who mean to murder love. There is nothing violent about it; no shock is given; Hope is not abruptly strangled, but merely dreams of evil, and fights with gradually stifling shadows. When the last convulsions come, they are not terrific; the frame has been weakened for dissolution; love dies like natural decay. It seems the kindest way of doing a cruel thing.

Old letters are the dreariest ghosts in the world, and you cannot keep more treacherous rubbish in your possession.

The woman seeking for an anomaly wants a master.

Words big in the mouth serve their turn when there is no way of satisfying the intelligence.

What is worthless if it be well looked at? Nay, the most worthless creatures are most serviceable for examination when the microscope is applied to them as a simple study of human mechanism.

Work is medicine. A truism! Truisms, whether they lie in the depths of thought or on the surface, are at any rate the pearls of experience.

It is sufficient for some men to know they are seen through, in order to turn away in loathing from her whom they have desired; when they do turn away, they not uncommonly turn, with a rush of old affection, to those who have generously trusted them in the days past, and blindly thought them estimable beings.

The young man who can look on them we call fallen women with a noble eye, is to my mind he that is most nobly begotten of the race, and likeliest to be the sire of a noble line.

The creature's soul had put no gloss upon her sin. She had sinned, and her suffering was manifest. She had chosen to stand up and take the scourge of God ; after which the stones cast by men are not painful. By this I mean that she had voluntarily stripped her spirit bare of evasion, and seen herself for what she was, pleading no excuse. His scourge is truth, and she had faced it.

THE precious metal, which is knowledge, sir, is only to be obtained by *mining* for it ; and that excellent occupation necessarily sends a man out of sight for a number of years.

ONE learns to have compassion for fools, by studying them ; and the fool, though Nature is wise, is next door to Nature.

SHE has the manners of a lady : a lady, I say, — not of the modern young lady, with whom, I am happy to say, she does not come into competition. She has not been sedulously trained to pull *her* way, when she is to go into harness with a yoke-fellow.

IMAGINATION misled the old man. There have been spotless reputations gained in the service of virtue before now, and chaste and beautiful persons have walked the narrow plank, envied and admired, and they have ultimately tottered and all but fallen, or they have quite fallen, from no worse incitement than curiosity. Cold curiosity, as the directors of our human constitution tell us, is, in the colder condition of our blood, a betraying vice, leading to sin at a period when the fruits of sin afford the smallest satisfaction. It is, in fact, our last probation, and one of our latest delusions. If that is passed successfully, we may really be pronounced of some worth.

CAN a man go farther than his nature? Never, when he takes passion on board. By other means his nature may be enlarged and nerved; but passion will find his weakness, and, while urging him on, will constantly betray him at that point.

VITTORIA.

VITTORIA.

HEADS, you illustrious young gentlemen, heads, not legs and arms, move a conspiracy.

IN the end, a country true to itself, and determined to claim God's gift to brave men, will overmatch a mere army, however solid its face. But an inspired energy of faith is demanded of it.

VITTORIA's spirit was in one of those angry knots which are half of the intellect, half of the will, and are much under the domination of one or other of the passions in the ascendant. She was resolved to go forward; she felt justified in going forward: but the divine afflatus of enthusiasm buoyed her no longer, and she required the support of all that accuracy of insight and senseless stubbornness which there might be in her nature. The feeling that it was she to whom it was given to lift the torch and plant the standard of Italy, had swept her as through the strings of a harp.

For when the soul of a youth can be heated above common heat, the vices of passion shrivel up and aid the purer flame.

Among the nobler order of women there is, when they plunge into strife, a craving for idealistic truths which men are apt, under the heat and hurry of their energies, to put aside as stars that are meant merely for shining.

A man may have good nerve to face the scene which he is certain will be enacted, who shrinks from an hour that is suspended in doubt.

The flattery of beholding a great assembly of human creatures bound glittering in wizard subservience to the voice of one soul, belongs to the artist, and is the cantatrice's glory, pre-eminent over whatever poor glory the world gives.

This is what the great voice does for us. It rarely astonishes our ears. It illumines our souls, as you see the lightning make the unintelligible darkness leap into long mountain-ridges, and twisting vales, and spires of cities, and inner recesses of light within light, rose-like, towards a central core of violet heat.

THE poetic definition of "now," is that it is a small boat, my daughter, in which the female heart is constantly pushing out to sea and sinking. "To-morrow" is an island in the deeps, where grain grows.

A GREAT voice is an ocean. You cannot drain it with forty thousand opera-hats. It is something found, — an addition to the wealth of life.

VITTORIA read the faces of the mornings as human creatures have tried to gather the sum of their destinies off changing surfaces, — fair not meaning fair, nor black black, but either the mask upon the secret of God's terrible will; and to learn it and submit, was the spiritual burden of her motherhood that the child leaping within her might live. Not to hope blindly in the exceeding anxiousness of her passionate love, nor blindly to fear; not to let her soul fly out among the twisting chances; not to sap her great maternal duty by affecting stoical serenity, — to nurse her soul's strength, and suckle her womanly weakness with the tears which are poison when repressed; to be at peace with a disastrous world for the sake of the dependent life unborn: by such pure efforts she clung to God. Soft dreams of sacred nuptial tenderness, tragic images, wild pity, were like phantoms enclosing her as she went; but they were beneath her feet, and she kept them from lodging between her breasts. The thought that her husband, though he should have perished, was not a life lost if their child lived, sustained her powerfully. . . . The mountains and the valleys scarce had names for her understanding; they were but a scene where the will of her Maker was at work. Rarely has a soul been so subjected by its own force. She certainly had the image of God in her mind.

OUR life is but a little holding, lent
To do a mighty labour. We are one
With Heaven and the stars when it is spent
To serve God's aim; else die we with the sun.

THE ADVENTURES OF HARRY RICHMOND.

THE

ADVENTURES OF HARRY RICHMOND.

ONE who has indulged his soul in invective will not, if he has power in his hand, be robbed of his climax with impunity, by a cool response that seems to trifle, and scourges.

I 'VE stopped my tongue all this while before a scoundrel 'd corkscrew the best-bottled temper right or left, go where you will, one end o' the world to the other.

HARK you, Mary Waddy, who 're a widdie, which 's as much as say, an unocc'pied mind, there 's Cockney, and there 's country, and there 's school. Mix the three, strain, and throw away the sediment.

JOHN THRESHER had a laborious mind; it cost him beads on his forehead to mount to these satisfactory heights of meditation. He told me once that he thought one's country was like one's wife: you were born in the first, and married to the second, and had to learn all about them afterwards, — ay, and make the best of them.

To hope and not be impatient is really to believe.

THERE is nothing like a pent-up secret of the heart for accumulating powers of speech, — I mean in youth. The mental distilling process sets in later, and then you have irony instead of eloquence.

WHEN you think long undividedly of a single object, it gathers light; and when you draw near it in person, the strange thing to your mind is the absence of that light.

BOYS are always putting down the ciphers of their observations of people beloved by them, but do not add up a sum-total.

For a princess who is no more than princess, her ancestors are a bundle of fagots, and she, with her mind and heart tied fast to them, is, at least a good half of her, dead wood.

We can err very easily in youth; and to find ourselves shooting at a false mark uncontrollably, must be a cruel thing. . . . For who beguiles so much as Self? Tell her to play, she plays her sweetest. Lurk to surprise her, and what a serpent she becomes! She is not to be aware that you are watching her. You have to review her acts, observe her methods. Always be above her; then by and by you catch her hesitating at cross-roads; then she is bare: you catch her bewailing or exulting; then she can no longer pretend she is other than she seems. I make Self the feminine, for she is the weaker, and the soul has to purify and raise her.

Now I ask [said Dr. Julius] whether you have a scheme of life, that I may know whether you are to be another of those huge human pumpkins, called rich men, who cover your country and drain its blood and intellect. Your nobles are nothing but rich men inflated with empty traditions of insufferable, because unwarrantable pride, and drawing substance from alliances with the merchant class. Are they your leaders? Do they lead you in letters? in the arts? ay, or in government? No, not — I am informed — not even in military service! And these our titled witlings do manage to hold up their brainless pates. You are all in one mass, struggling in the stream to get out, and lie, and wallow, and belch on the banks. You work so hard that you have all but one aim, and that is fatness and ease!

"You worship your aristocracy," went on the German Professor, "it is notorious. You have a sort of sagacity. . . . You worship your so-called aristocracy perforce, in order to preserve an ideal of contrast to the vulgarity of the nation."

Astronomers condescending to earthly philosophy may admit that advance in the physical universe is computable, though not perceptible. Somewhither we tend, shell and spirit. You English, fighting your little battles of domestic policy, and sneering at us for flying at higher game, — you unimpressionable English, who won't believe in the existence of aims that don't drop on the ground before your eyes, and squat and stare at you, — you assert that man's labor is completed when the poor are kept from crying out.

Now my question is, Have you a scheme of life consonant with the spirit of modern philosophy, — with the views of intelligent, moral, humane beings of this period? Or are you one of your robust English brotherhood, worthy of Caligula in his prime, lions in gymnastics — for a time ; *sheep* always in the dominions of mind ; and all of one pattern, all in a rut !

AIM your head at a star — your head ! — and even if you miss it you don't fall. It's that light dancer, that gambler, the heart in you, my good young man, which aims itself at inaccessible heights, and has the fall — somewhat icy to reflect on ! It's a mind that wins a mind.

The bone and marrow of study form the surest antidote to the madness of that light gambler, the heart.

The world has accurate eyes, if they are not very penetrating. The world will see a want of balance immediately, and also too true a balance, but it will not detect a depth of concord between two souls that do not show some fretfulness on the surface.

If a man's fate were as a forbidden fruit, detached from him, and in front of him, he might hesitate fortunately before plucking it; but, as most of us are aware, the vital half of it lies in the seed paths he has traversed.

We are sons of yesterday, not of the morning. The past is our mortal mother, no dead thing. Our future constantly reflects her to the soul. Nor is it ever the new man of to-day who grasps his future, good or ill. We are pushed to it by the hundreds of days we have buried eager ghosts. And if you have not the habit of taking counsel with them, you are but an instrument in their hands.

A MAN'S review of the course of his life grows for a moment stringently serious, when he beholds the stream broadening perchance under the light.

EXCELLENT is pride; but oh! be sure of its foundations before you go on building monument high. I know nothing to equal the anguish of an examination of the basis of one's pride that discovers it not solidly fixed; an imposing, self-imposing structure, piled upon empty cellarage. . . . A man's pride is the front and head-piece of his character, his soul's support or snare.

I HAVE to thank the interminable hours on my wretched sick-bed for a singularly beneficial investigation of the ledger of my deeds and omissions and moral stock.

NOTHING but poetry makes romances passable; for poetry is the everlastingly and embracingly human. Without it your fictions are flat foolishness, non-nourishing substance, — a species of brandy and gruel!—diet for craving stomachs that can support nothing solider, and must have the weak stuff stiffened.

ONE would like possibly, after expulsion out of Eden, to climb the gates to see how the trees grow there.

ONE who consents to live as I had done, in a hope and a retrospect, will find his life slipping between the two, like the ships under the striding Colossus.

PARSONS and petticoats must always mince the meat to hash the fact.

THE contemplation of the curious littleness of the lives of men and women lived in this England of ours, made me feel as if I looked at them out of a palace balcony-window; for no one appeared to hope very much or to fear; people trotted in their different kinds of harness. . . . An existence without colour, without anxious throbbings, without salient matter for thought, challenged contempt.

Puns are the small-pox of the language; we're cursed with an epidemic. By gad! the next time I meet him I'll roar out for vaccine matter.

The stultification of one's feelings and ideas in circumstances which divide and set them at variance is worse than positive pain.

My strivings were against my leanings; and imagining the latter, which involved no sacrifice of the finer sense of honour, to be in the direction of my lower nature, I repelled them to preserve a lofty aim that led me through questionable ways.

Egoism is not peculiar to any period of life; it is only especially curious in a young man beginning to match himself against his elders, for in him it suffuses the imagination; he is not merely selfishly sentient, or selfishly scheming; his very conceptions are selfish.

In my time, all young gentlemen were born Tories. The doctor no more expected to see a Radical come into the world from a good family than a radish.

This looking at the roots of yourself, if you are possessed of a nobler half that will do it, is a sound corrective of an excessive ambition.

Carry your fever to the Alps, you of minds diseased; not to sit down in sight of them ruminating, for bodily ease and comfort will trick the soul and set you measuring our lean humanity against yonder sublime and infinite; but mount, rack the limbs, wrestle it out among the peaks; taste danger, sweat, earn rest; learn to discover ungrudgingly, that haggard fatigue is the fair vision you have run to earth, and that rest is your uttermost reward. Would you know what it is to hope again, and have all your hopes at hand?—hang upon the crags at a gradient that makes your next step a debate between the thing you are and the thing you may become. There the many little hopes grow for the climber, like flowers and food, immediate, prompt to prove their uses, sufficient if just within the grasp, as mortal hopes should be. Now the old lax life closes in about you there! You are the man of your faculties, nothing more. Why should a man pretend to be more? We ask it wonderingly when we are healthy. Poetic rhapsodists in the vale below may tell you of the joy and grandeur of the upper regions, they cannot pluck you the medical herb. He gets that for himself who wanders the marshy ledge at nightfall to behold the distant Sennhüttchen twinkle, who leaps the green-eyed crevasses, and in the solitude of an emerald alp stretches a salt hand to the mountain kine.

To kill the deer and be sorry for the suffering wretch is common.

THE moods of half-earnest men and feeble lovers narrowly escape the farcical.

Is it any waste of time to write of love? The trials of life are in it, but in a narrow ring and a fierier. You may learn to know yourself through love, as you do after years of life, whether you are fit to lift them that are about you, or whether you are but a cheat and a load on the backs of your fellows. The impure perishes, the inefficient languishes, the moderate comes to its autumn of decay — these are of the kinds which aim at satisfaction to die of it soon or late. The love that survives has strangled craving; it lives because it lives to nourish and succour like the heavens.

But to strangle craving is indeed to go through a death before you reach your immortality.

THE EGOIST.

THE EGOIST.

Most of the people one has at a dinner-table are drums. A rub-a-dub-dub on them is the only way to get a sound. When they can be persuaded to do it upon one another, they call it conversation.

Strange eclipse, when the hue of truth comes shadowing over our bright ideal planet. It will not seem the planet's fault, but truth's. Reality is the offender; delusion our treasure that we are robbed of. Then begins with us the term of wilful delusion, and its necessary accompaniment of the disgust of reality.

She said, " I must be myself to be of any value to you, Willoughby." She would not burn the world for him; she would not, though a purer poetry is little imaginable, reduce herself to ashes, or incense or essence, in honor of him, and so, by love's transmutation, literally be the man she was to marry. She preferred to be herself, with the egoism of woman!

THE language of the primitive sentiments of men is of the same expression at all times, minus the primitive colours when a modern gentleman addresses his lady.

CYNICISM is intellectual dandyism without the coxcomb's feathers.

THE world has faults; glaciers have crevasses, mountains have chasms; but is not the effect of the whole sublime?

MEN whose pride is their backbone suffer convulsions where other men are barely aware of a shock.

SHE conceived the state of marriage with him [Sir Willoughby] as that of a woman tied, not to a

man of heart, but to an obelisk lettered all over
with hieroglyphics, and everlastingly hearing him
expound them, relishingly renewing his lectures on
them.

"THE ideal of conduct for women is to subject
their minds to the part of an accompaniment."

THE love-season is the carnival of egoism, and
it brings the touchstone to our natures. I speak of
love, not the mask, and not of the flutings upon
the theme of love, but of the passion; a flame
having, like our mortality, death in it as well as life,
that may or may not be lasting.

IN the hundred and fourth chapter of the thir-
teenth volume of the "Book of Egoism," it is written, "*Possession without obligation to the object
possessed approaches felicity.*"

It is the rarest condition of ownership. For
example: the possession of land is not without
obligation both to the soil and tax-collector; the
possession of fine clothing is oppressed by obliga-

tion; gold, jewelry, works of art, enviable household furniture, are positive fetters; the possession of a wife we find surcharged with obligation. In all these cases possession is a gentle term for enslavement, bestowing the sort of felicity attained to by the helot drunk. You can have the joy, the pride, the intoxication of possession: you can have no free soul. But there is one instance of possession, and that the most perfect, which leaves us free, under not a shadow of obligation, receiving ever, never giving, or if giving, giving only of our waste; as it were, by form of perspiration, radiation, if you like; unconscious poral bountifulness; and it is a beneficent process for the system. Our possession of an adoring female's worship is this instance. The soft cherishable Parsee is hardly at any season other than prostrate. She craves nothing save that you continue in being, — her sun,—which is your firm constitutional endeavor, and thus you have a most exact alliance; she supplying spirit to your matter, while at the same time presenting matter to your spirit, verily a comfortable apposition. The Gods do bless it.

The beauty of laws for human creatures is their adaptability to new stitching.

Quick natures run out to calamity in any little shadow of it flung before. Terrors of apprehension drive them. They stop not short of the uttermost when they are on the wings of dread. A frown means tempest, a wind wreck; to see fire is to be seized by it.

Maidens are commonly reduced to read the masters of their destinies by their instincts.

We do not with impunity abandon the initiative. Men who have yielded it are like cavalry put on the defensive; a very small force with an ictus will scatter them.

The slave of a passion thinks in a ring, as hares run; he will cease where he began.

Women have us back to the conditions of primitive man, or they shoot us higher than the topmost star. But it is as we please. Let them tell us what we are to them; for us they are our back and front of life; the poet's Lesbia, the poet's Beatrice; ours is the choice. And were it proved that some of the bright things are in the pay of Darkness, with the stamp of his coin on their palms, and that some are the very angels we hear sung of, not the less might we say that they find us out, they have us by our leanings. They are to us what we hold of best or worst within. By their state is our civilization judged; and if it is hugely animal still, that is because primitive men abound and will have their pasture. Since the lead is ours, the leaders must bow their heads to the sentence.

JEALOUSY of a woman is the primitive egoism seeking to refine in a blood gone to savagery under apprehension of an invasion of rights; it is in action the tiger threatened by a rifle, when his paw is rigid on quick flesh; he tears the flesh for rage at the intruder. The Egoist, who is our original male in giant form, had no bleeding victim beneath his paw, but there was the sex to mangle.

YOUNG women are trained to cowardice. For them to front an evil with plain speech is to be guilty of effrontery, and forfeit the waxen polish of purity, and therewith their commanding place in the market. They are trained to please man's taste, for which purpose they soon learn to live out of themselves, and look on themselves as he looks. Without courage, conscience is a sorry guest; and if all goes well with the pirate captain, conscience will be made to walk the plank for being of no service to either party.

THE strict man of honour plays a part that he should not reflect on till about the fall of the curtain, otherwise he will be likely sometimes to feel the shiver of foolishness at his good conduct.

IN the first gush of our wisdom drawn directly from experience there is a mortal intoxication that cancels the old world and establishes a new one, not allowing us to ask whether it is too late.

PATHOS is a tide; often it carries the awakener of it off his feet, and whirls him over and over, armour and all, in ignominious attitudes of helpless prostration, whereof he may well be ashamed in the retrospect. We cannot quite preserve our dignity when we stoop to the work of calling forth tears. Moses had probably to take a nimble jump away from the rock after that venerable lawgiver had knocked the water out of it.

THE man who can be a friend is the man who will presume to be a censor.

THERE are times when there is no medicine for us in sages, we want slaves; we scorn to temporize, we must overbear.

IF we are not to be beloved, spare us the small coin of compliments on character.

CLEVERNESS in women is not uncommon. Intellect is the pearl. A woman of intellect is as good as a Greek statue; she is divinely wrought, and she is divinely rare.

THE hero of two women must die and be wept over in common before they can appreciate one another.

AT a certain age our teachers are young people; we learn by looking backward.

ESTEEM 's a mellow thing, that comes after bloom and fire, like an evening at home.

A ROUGH truth, madam, I should define to be that description of truth which is not imparted to mankind without a powerful impregnation of the roughness of the teller.

A TRIED steadfast woman is the one jewel of the sex. She points to her husband like the sunflower; her love illuminates him; she lives in him, for him; she testifies to his worth; she drags the world to his feet; she leads the chorus of his praises; she justifies him in his own esteem. Surely there is not on earth such beauty.

Who are not fools to be set spinning, if we choose to whip them with their vanity! It is the consolation of the great to watch them spin.

To be loved is to feel our littleness, hollowness, — feel shame. We come out in all our spots.

BEAUCHAMP'S CAREER.

BEAUCHAMP'S CAREER.

BEAUCHAMPISM, as one confronting him calls it, may be said to stand for nearly everything which is the obverse of Byronism, and rarely woos your sympathy, shuns the statuesque pathetic, or any kind of posturing. For Beauchamp will not even look at happiness to mourn its absence; melodious lamentations, demoniacal scorn, are quite alien to him. His faith is in working and fighting. With every inducement to offer himself for a romantic figure, he despises the pomades and curling-irons of modern romance, its shears and its labels: in fine, every one of those positive things by whose aid, and by some adroit flourishing of them, the nimbus known as a mysterious halo is produced about a gentleman's head. ... We are all given to lose our solidity and fly at it; although the faithful mirror of fiction has been showing us latterly that a too superhuman beauty has disturbed popular belief in the bare beginnings of the existence of heroes; but this very likely is nothing more than a fit of Republicanism in the nursery, and a deposition of the leading doll for lack of variety in him. That conqueror of circumstances will, as the dullest soul may begin predicting, return on his cock-horse to favour and authority.

Meantime, the exhibition of a hero whom circumstances overcome, and who does not weep or ask you for a tear, who continually forfeits attractiveness by declining to better his own fortunes, must run the chances of a novelty during the interregnum.

———

CONVICTIONS are generally first impressions sealed with later prejudices.

———

IF you meddle with politics, you must submit to be held up on the prongs of a fork, my boy, soaped by your backers and shaved by the foe.

———

IT happens in war as in wit, that all birds of wonder fly to a flaring reputation. He that has done one wild thing must necessarily have done the other.

THE winter was dreadful: every kind heart that went to bed with cold feet felt acutely for our soldiers on the frozen heights, and thoughts of heroes were as good as warming pans.

A BONE in a boy's mind for him to gnaw and worry, corrects the vagrancies and promotes the healthy activities, whether there be marrow in it or not. Supposing it furnishes only dramatic entertainment in that usually vacant tenement or powder-shell, it will be of service.

THERE's a pitch and tar in politics as well as on shipboard.

ROSAMOND noticed the peculiarity of the books he selected for his private reading. They were not boy's books, books of adventure and the like. His favorite author was one writing of Heroes in (so she esteemed it) a style resembling either early architecture or utter dilapidation, so loose and rough it seemed; a wind-in-the-orchard style, that tumbled down here and there an appreciable fruit with uncouth bluster; sentences without commencements running to abrupt endings and smoke, like waves against a sea-wall, learned dictionary words giving a hand to street slang, and accents falling on them haphazard, like slant rays from driving clouds; all the pages in a breeze, the whole book producing a kind of electrical agitation in the mind and the joints. . . . He had dug the book out of a bookseller's shop in Malta, captivated by its title, and had, since the day of his purchase, gone at it again and again, *getting nibbles of golden meaning by instalments*, as with a solitary pick in a very dark mine, until the illumination of an idea struck him that there was a great deal more in the book than there was in himself.

As for titles, the way to defend them is to be worthy of them.

THE future not being born, my friend, we will abstain from baptizing it.

LETTERS of a lover in an extremity of love, crying for help, are as curious to cool strong men as the contortions of the proved heterodox tied to a stake must have been to their chastening clerical judges.

THERE is a pause between the descent of a diver and his return to the surface, when those who would not have him forgotten by the better world above him do rightly to relate anecdotes of him, if they can, and to provoke laughter at him. The encouragement of the humane sense of superiority over an object of interest which laughter gives, is good for the object; and besides, if you begin to tell sly stories of one in the deeps, who is holding his breath to fetch a pearl or two for you all, you divert a particular sympathetic oppression of the chest, that the extremely sensitive are apt to suffer from, and you dispose the larger number to keep in mind a person they no longer see. Otherwise it is likely that he will, very shortly after he has made his plunge, fatigue the contemplative brains above, and be shuffled off them, even as great ocean smooths away the dear vanished man's immediate circle of foam, and rapidly confounds the rippling memory of him with its other agitations. And in such a case the apparition of his head upon our common level once more will almost certainly cause a disagreeable shock; nor is it improbable that his first natural snorts in his native element, though they be simply to obtain his share of the health of life, will draw down on him condemnation for eccentric behaviour and unmannerly; and this in spite of the jewel he brings, unless it be an exceedingly splendid one. The reason is, that our brave world cannot pardon a breach of continuity for any petty bribe.

No man ever did hard work who held counsel with his family. The family view of a man's fit conduct is the weak point of the country. It is no other view than "Better thy condition for our sakes." Ha! In this way we breed sheep, fatten oxen; men are dying off. Resolution taken to consult the family, means—waste your time! Those who go to it want an excuse for altering their minds. The family view is everlastingly the shopkeeper's. Purse, Pence, Ease, increase of worldly goods, personal importance, the Pound, the English

Pound! Dare do *that*, and you forfeit your share of Port wine in this world: you won't be dubbed with a title; you'll be fingered at! Lord, Lord, is it the region *inside* a man, or out, that gives him peace? *Out*, they say, for they have lost faith in the existence of an inner. They haven't it. Air sucker, blood pump, cooking machinery, and a battery of trained instincts, aptitudes, fill up their vacuum.

THE wretched tinkler called a piano, which tries at the whole orchestra and murders every instrument in the attempt, is like our modern civilization,— a taming and a diminishing of individuals for an insipid harmony.

MAN's aim has hitherto been to keep men from having a soul for *this* world.

IT will be found a common case, that when we have yielded to our instincts, and then have to soothe conscience, we must slaughter somebody for a sacrificial offering to our sense of comfort.

LIKE most men who have little to say, he was an orator in print; but that was a poor medium for him, — his body without his fire.

DELICIOUS and rapturous effects are to be produced in the flood of a Liberal oration by a chance infusion of the fierier spirit a flavour of Radicalism. That is the thing to set an audience bounding and quirking. Whereas, if you commence by tilting a Triton pitcher full of the neat liquor upon them, you have to resort to the natural element for the orator's art of variation, — you are diluted, and that's bathos.

THE Radical orator has but two notes, and one is the drawling pathetic, and the other the ultra furious; and the effect of the former we liken to the English workingman's wife's hot-set queasy brew of well-meant villany, that she calls by the innocent name of tea; and the latter is to be blown, asks to be blown, and never should be blown without at least seeming to be blown, with an accompaniment of a house on fire.

When hear you a thrilling Tory speech that carries the country with it, save when the incendiary Radical has shrieked?

The address was admirably worded, sir, I make bold to say it; but most indubitably it threatened powerful drugs for weak stomachs, and it blew cold on votes, which are sensitive plants like nothing else in botany.

The infant candidate delights in his honesty, like the babe in its nakedness, the beautiful virgin in her innocence.

A dash of conventionalism makes the whole civilized world kin.

Beauchamp was dropped by the *Esperanza's* boat near Otley Ferry, to walk along the beach to Bevisham, and he kept an eye on the elegant vessel as she glided swan-like to her moorings off Mount Laurel's park, through merchant craft, colliers, and trawlers, loosely shaking her towering snow-white sails, unchallenged in her scornful supremacy,— an image of a refinement of beauty, and of a beautiful servicelessness.

As the yacht, so the mistress; things of wealth, owing their graces to wealth, devoting them to wealth, — splendid achievements of art both! and dedicated to the gratification of the superior senses. Say they were precious examples of an accomplished civilization; and perhaps they did offer a visible ideal of grace for the rough world to aim at. They might in the abstract address a bit of a monition to the uncultivated, and encourage the soul to strive toward perfection in beauty; and there is no contesting the value of beauty when the soul is taken into account. But were they not in too great a profusion in proportion to their utility? That was the question for Nevil Beauchamp. The democratic spirit inhabitating him, temporarily or permanently, asked whether they were not increasing to numbers which were oppressive. And, further, whether it was good for the country, the race, ay, the species, that they should be so distinctly removed from the thousands who fought the grand, and the grisly, old battle with nature for bread of life. Those grimy sails of the colliers and fishing-smacks, set them in a great sea, would have beauty for eye and soul beyond that of elegance and refinement. And do but look at them thoughtfully, the poor are everlastingly, unrelievedly, in the abysses of the great sea.

DID Beauchamp at all desire to have those idly lovely adornments of riches, the yacht and the lady, swept away? Oh dear no! He admired them, he was at home with them. They were much to his taste. . . . Beauty plucked the heart from his breast. But he had taken up arms; he had drunk of the *questioning* cup, that which denieth peace to us, and projects us upon the missionary search of the *How*, the *Wherefore*, and the *Why Not*, ever afterward.

He questioned his justification and yours, for gratifying tastes in an ill-regulated world of wrongdoing, suffering, sin, and bounties unrighteously dispensed, — not sufficiently dispersed. He said by and by to pleasure, battle to-day. From his point of observation, and with the store of ideas and images his fiery yet reflective youth had gathered, he presented himself, as it were, saddled to that hard-riding force known as the logical impetus, which, spying its quarry over precipices, across oceans and deserts, and through systems and webs and into shops and cabinets of costliest china, will come at it, will not be refused, let the distances and the breakages be what they may. He went, like the meteoric man with the mechanical legs in the song, too quick for a cry of protestations, and reached results amazing to his instincts, his tastes, and his training not less rapidly and naturally than tremendous. Ergo is shot forth from the clash of a syllogism.

THERE's always danger in disunion. That's what the rich won't see. They see simply nothing out of their own circle; and they won't take a thought of the overpowering contrast between their luxury, and the way of living, that's half starving, of the poor. They understand it when fever comes up from back alleys and cottages, and then they join their efforts to sweep the poor out of the district. The poor are to get their work anyhow, after a long morning's walk over the prescribed space; for we must have poor, you know. The wife of a parson I canvassed yesterday said to me,

"Who is to work for us if you do away with the poor, Captain Beauchamp?"

I HAVE heard that man say that the Church stands to show the passion of the human race for the drama. . . . He calls the Protestant clergy the social police of the English middle class. . . . He has sharp eyes for the sins of the poor. As for the rich, they support his church, they listen to his sermon — to set an example.

IT 's put down to the wickedness of human nature, that the parson has not got hold of the people. The parsons have lost them by a senseless Conservatism, because they look to the Tories for the support of their church, and let the religion run down the gutters.

EARNESTNESS works out its own cure more surely than frenzy.

CONCEIVE, for the fleeting instants permitted to such insufferable flights of fancy, our picked men ruling! So despotic an oligarchy as would be there is not a happy subject of contemplation. It is not too much to say that a domination of the Intellect in England would at once and entirely alter the face of the country. We should be governed by the head with a vengeance; all the rest of the country being base members indeed,—Spartans' helots. Criticism, now so helpful to us, would wither to the root; fun would die out of Parliament, and outside of it; we could never laugh at our masters or command them.

Do you not hear in imagination the land's regrets for that amiable nobility whose pretensions were comically built on birth, acres, style, and an air? . . . At present I believe it to be their honest opinion, common to a majority of them, that it is more salutary besides more diverting to have the fools of the kingdom represented than not. . . . That would be an inaccessible tyranny of a very small minority, necessarily followed by tremendous convulsions.

CONGHAM also, Congham had passed through his Radical phase, as one does on the road to wisdom. So the frog telleth tadpoles: he too has wriggled most preposterous of tails; and he has shoved a circular flat head into corners unadapted to its shape; and that the undeveloped one should dutifully listen to experience, and accept guidance, is devoutly to be hoped.

A CLOUD of millinery shoots me off a mile from a woman.

IF you have a nation politically corrupt, you won't have a good state of morals in it, and the laws that keep society together bear upon the politics of a country.

WOMEN don't care uncommonly for the men who love them, though they like precious well to be loved.

A THOROUGHLY good-looking girl, who takes to a fellow for what he's doing in the world, must have ideas of him precious different from the adoration of six feet three and a fine seat in the saddle.

I SAY that the education for women is to teach them to rely on themselves.

THE slavery of the love of a woman chained like Renée, was the most revolting of prospects to a man who cherished his freedom that he might work to the end of time. . . . Her presence resembled those dark sunsets throwing the spell of colour across the world; when there is no question with us of morning or of night, but of that sole splendour only.

RENÉE'S gift of speech counted unnumbered strings, which she played on with a grace that clothed the skill, and was her natural endowment,— an art perfected by the education of the world. Who cannot talk! but who can? Discover the writers in a day when all are writing! It is as rare an art as poetry, and in the mouths of women as enrapturing, richer than their voices in music.

LANGUAGE flowed from Renée in affinity with the pleasure-giving laws that make the curves we recognize as beauty in sublimer arts.

WOULD you, that are separable from boys and mobs, and the object malignly called the Briton, prefer the celestial singing of a woman to her excellently talking? But not if it were given you to run in unison with her genius of the tongue, following her verbal ingenuities and feminine silk flashes of meaning; not if she led you to match her fine, quick perceptions with more or less of the discreet concordance of the violoncello accompanying the viol.

NAME the two countries which alone have produced *The Woman*, the ideal woman, the woman of art, whose beauty, grace, and wit offer her to our contemplation in an atmosphere above the ordinary conditions of the world: these two countries are France and Greece. None other give you the perfect woman, the woman who conquers time, as she conquers men, by virtue of the divinity in her blood; and she, as little as illustrious heroes, is to be judged by the laws and standards of lesser creatures. In fashioning her, nature and art have worked together; in her, poetry walks the earth.

OLD love reviving may be love of a phantom, after all. We can, if it must revive, keep it to the limits of a ghostly love.

You may start a sermon from stones to hit the stars.

He must be a practised orator who shall descend out of the abstract to take up a heavy lump of the concrete.

Note, then, that Radicals, always marching to the triumph, never taste it; and for Tories it is Dead Sea fruit, ashes in their mouths! Those Liberals, those temporizers, compromisers, a concourse of atoms! glorify themselves in the animal satisfaction of sucking the juice of the fruit, for which they pay with their souls. They have no true cohesion, for they have no vital principle.

Cowardice is even worse for nations than for individual men.

May not one love, not craving to be beloved? Such a love does not sap our pride, but supports it; increases rather than diminishes our noble self-esteem. To attain such a love the martyrs writhed up to the crown of saints.

ONE may venerate old families when they show the blood of the founder.

THAT is no aristocracy, if it does not head the people in virtue, — military, political, national; I mean the qualities required by the times for leadership.

ONE may be as a weed of the sea while one's fate is being decided. To love is to be on the sea, out of sight of land.

GLORIOUS, and solely glorious love, that has risen above emotion, quite independent of craving! That is to be the bird of upper air, poised on his wings. It is a home in the sky.

ON with your mission, and never a summing of results in hand, nor thirst for prospects, nor counting upon harvests; for seed sown in faith day by day is the nightly harvest of the soul, — and with the soul we work, with the soul we see.

DESIRES to realize our gains are akin to the passion of usury; these are tricks of the usurer to grasp his gold in act and imagination.

"Work at the people." At them, remark!—Moveless do they seem to you? Why, so is the earth to the sowing husbandman, and though we cannot forecast a reaping season, we have in history durable testification that our seasons come in the souls of men, yea, as a planet that we have set in motion, and faster and faster are we spinning it, and firmer and firmer shall we set it to regularity of revolution.

Professors, prophets, masters, each hitherto has had his creed and system to offer, good mayhap for the term; and each has put it forth for the truth everlasting, to drive the dagger to the heart of time, and put the axe to human growth! That one circle of wisdom, issuing of the experience and needs of their day, should act the despot over all other circles forever! So where at first light shone to light the yawning frog to his wet ditch, there with the necessitated revolution of men's minds in the course of ages darkness radiates.

His insensibility to music was curious, considering how impressionable he was to verse and to songs of birds. He listened with an oppressed look, as to something the particular secret of which had to be reached by a determined effort of sympathy for those whom it affected. He liked it, if she did, and said he liked it, reiterated that he liked it, clearly trying hard to comprehend it, as unmoved by the swell and sigh of the resonant brass as a man could be, while her romantic spirit thrilled to it, and was beautiful in glowing visions and in tenderness.

SHE was one of the artificial creatures called women, who dare not be spontaneous, and cannot act independently if they would continue to be admirable in the world's eye, and who, for that object, must remain fixed on shelves, like other marketable wares, avoiding motion to avoid shattering or tarnishing. This is their fate, only in degree less inhuman than that of Hellenic and Trojan princesses offered up to the Gods, or pretty slaves to the dealers.

THE children of wealth and the children of the sun alike believe that Providence is for them, and it would seem that the former can do without it less than the latter, though the former are less inclined to give it personification.

DECIDEDLY Cecilia was a more beautiful woman than Renée; but on which does the eye linger longest,—which draws the heart? a radiant landscape when the tall, ripe wheat flashes between shadow and shine in the stately march of summer, or the peep into dewy woodland on to dark water?

DARK-EYED Renée was not beauty, but attraction; she touched the double chords within us which are we know not whether harmony or discord, but a divine discord if an uncertified harmony beyond plain sweetness or majesty.

THERE are touches of bliss in anguish that superhumanize bliss, touches of mystery in simplicity, of the eternal in the variable.

GHASTLY as a minority is in an election, in a life-long struggle it is refreshing and encouraging. The young world and its triumph is with the majority.

WE who interpret things heavenly by things earthly, must not hope to juggle with them for our pleasures, and can look to no absolution of evil acts.

AN incessant struggle of one man with the world, which position usually ranks his relatives against him, does not conduce to soundness of judgment.

THE world in motion is not so wise that it can pretend to silence the outcry of an ordinarily generous heart even, — the very infant of antagonism to its methods and establishments.

HE really respected Cecilia: it is not too much to say that he worshipped her with the devout worship rendered to the ideal Englishwoman by the heart of the nation. For him she was purity, charity, the keeper of the keys of whatsoever is held precious by men; she was a midway saint, a light between day and darkness, in whom the spirit in the flesh shone like the growing star amid thin, sanguine colour, the sweeter, the brighter, the more translucent, the longer known. And if the image will allow it, the nearer down to him the holier she seemed.

The slumberer roused in darkness by the relentless, insane-seeming bell which hails him to duty, melts at the charms of sleep, and feels that logic is with him in his preference of his pillow; but the tireless, revolving world outside, nature's pitiless antagonist, has hung one of its balances about him, and his actions are directed by the state of the scales, wherein duty weighs deep and desirability swings like a pendent doll.

Conscious rectitude, too, after the pattern of the well-behaved Æneas, quitting the fair bosom of Carthage in obedience to the Gods, for an example to his Roman progeny, might have stiffened his backbone and put a crown upon his brows.

The rich love the nation through their possessions, otherwise they have no country. If they loved the country, they would care for the people.

Their hearts are eaten up by property. . . . This flood of luxury is the body's drunkenness and the soul's death.

THE world and nature, which are opposed in relation to our vital interests, each agrees to demand of us a perfect victory, on pain otherwise of proving it a stage performance ; and the victory over the world, as over nature, is over self ; and this victory lies in yielding perpetual service to the world and none to nature ; for the world has to be wrought out, nature to be subdued.

WHEN life rolls back on us after the long ebb of illness, little whispers and diminutive images of the old joys and prizes of life arrest and fill our hearts.

A ROUGH man of rare quality civilizing under various influences, and half ludicrous, a little irritating, wholly estimable, has frequently won the benign approbation of the sex.

THE fact is, Beauchamp has no bend in him. He can't meet a man without trying to wrestle, and as long as he keeps his stiffness he believes he has won. I've heard an oculist say that the eye that does n't blink ends in blindness, and he who wont bend breaks.

———

But thirst is not enjoyment, and a satiated thirst that we insist on over-satisfying to drown the recollection of past anguish is baneful to the soul.

———

Most of our spiritual guides neglect the root to trim the flower.

———

The aim at an ideal life closely approaches, or easily inclines, to self-worship.

———

Sailing the sea on a cruise was like the gazing at wonderful colours of a western sky, — an oblivion of earthly dates and obligations. What mattered it that there were gales in August? She loved the sea, and the stinging salt spray, and circling gull, and plunging gannet, the sun on the waves, and the torn cloud.

———

These English, huddling more and more in flocks, turning to lumps, getting to be cut in a

pattern and marked by a label, — how they bark
and snap to rend an obnoxious original.

SOUND sleep, like hearty dining, endows men
with a sense of rectitude, and sunlight following
the former, as a pleasant spell of conversational
ease or sweet music the latter, smiles a celestial
approval of the performance.

WE women can read men by their power to love.
Where love exists, there is goodness.

THE pale flower of imagination, fed by dews,
not by sunshine, was born drooping, and hung
secret in her bosom, shy of a bell of the frail
wood-sorrel.

MEN who do not live in the present chiefly, but
hamper themselves with giant tasks in excess of
alarm for the future, however devoted and noble
they may be, — and he is an example of one that
is, — reduce themselves to the dimensions of pyg-
mies, they have the cry of infants. You reply,

Foresight is an element of love of country and mankind. But how often is not the foresight guesswork?

WHEN he was away and winds blew, the clouds which obscured an embracing imagination of him — such as, to be true and full and sufficient, should stretch like the dome of heaven over the humblest lives under contemplation — broke, and revealed him to her as one in mid-career, in mid-forest, who by force of character, advancing in self-conquest, strikes his impress right and left around him, because of his aim at stars.

ALAS for us ! — this our awful baggage in the rear of humanity, these women who have not moved on their own feet one step since the primal mother taught them to suckle, are perpetually pulling us backward on the march. Slaves of custom, forms, shows, and superstitions, they are slaves of the priests. . . . They are so in gratitude perchance, as the matter works. For at one period the priests did cherish and protect the weak from animal man.

But we have entered a broader daylight now, when the sun of high heaven has crowned our structure with the flower of brain. . . . Must we still be grinning subserviently to ancient usages and stale forms, because of a baggage that is, woe to us! too true, and we cannot cut ourselves loose from?

MY experience of the priest in our country is that he has abandoned — he's dead against — the only cause that can justify and keep up a church; the cause of the poor, the people. . . . He's against the cause of the people. Very well; I make my protest to the death against him. When he's a *Christian* instead of a *Churchman*, then may my example not be followed.

THERE's neither spiritual nor political brightness in England, but a common resolution to eat of good things and stick to them.

THE creed that rose in heaven sets below; and where we had an angel we have claw-feet and fangs. . . . The creed is much what it was when the followers diverged it from the Founder. But humanity is not *where* it was when that creed was food and guidance. Creeds will not die not fighting. We cannot root them up out of us without blood.

Ours is the belief that humanity advances beyond the limits of creeds, is to be tied to none. We reverence the Master in his teaching; we behold the limits of him in his creed, and that is not his work. We truly are his disciples, who see how far it was in him to do service; not they that made of his creed a strait-jacket for humanity.

In our prayers we dedicate the world to God, not calling him great for a title. No,—showing him we know him great in a limitless world, lord of a truth we tend to, have not grasped.

Prayer is good. I counsel it to you again and again, in joy, in sickness of heart. The infidel will

not pray; the creed slave prays to the image in
his box.

We make prayer a part of us, praying for no
gifts, no interventions, through the faith in prayer
opening the soul to the undiscerned. And take
this, my Beauchamp, for the good in prayer, —
that it makes us repose on the unknown with confidence, makes us flexible to change, makes us
ready for revolution, — for life then!

He who has the fountain of prayer in him will
not complain of hazards. Prayer is the recognition
of laws; the soul's exercise and source of strength;
its thread of conjunction with them. Prayer for
an object is the cajolery of an idol; the resource of
superstition. . . . We that fight the living world
must have the universal for succour of the truth in
it. Cast forth the soul in prayer, you meet the
effluence of the outer truth, you join with the
creative elements giving health to you; and that
crust of habit which is the soul's tomb: and custom,
the soul's tyrant; and pride, our volcano-peak, that
sinks us in a crater; and fear, which plucks the

feathers from the wings of the soul, and sets it shivering in a vault;—you are free of them; you live in the day and for the future by this exercise and discipline of the soul's faith. Us it keeps young everlastingly.

The religion of this vast English middle class ruling the land is Comfort. It is their central thought, their idea of necessity, their sole aim. Whatsoever ministers to comfort, seems to belong to it, pretends to support it, they yield their passive worship to. Whatsoever alarms it they join to crush. There you get at their point of unity.

Look to the truth in you, and deliver it with no afterthought of hope, for hope is dogged by dread; we give our courage as hostage for the fulfilment of what we hope.

Service is the noble office on earth, and when kings do service let them take the first honors of the state.

The English middle class, which has absorbed the upper, and despises, when it is not quaking before it, the lower, will have nothing above it but a rickety ornament like that you see on a confectioner's twelfth-cake.

9

THE TRAGIC COMEDIANS.

THE TRAGIC COMEDIANS.

An opinion formed by a woman is inflexible; the fact is not half so stubborn.

Men and women alike, who renounce their own individuality by cowering abjectly under some other before the storm, are in reality abjuring their idea of that other, and offering themselves up to the genius of Power, in whatsoever direction it may chance to be manifested, in whatsoever person. We no sooner shut our eyes than we consent to be prey, we lose the soul of election.

To ask if it was love is useless. Love may be celestial fire before it enters into the systems of mortals. It will then take the character of its place of abode, and we have to look not so much for the pure thing as for the passion.

ACTION means life to the soul as to the body. Compromise is virtual death; it is the pact between cowardice and comfort, under the title of expediency. So do we gather dead matter about us. So are we gradually self-stifled, corrupt. The war with evil in every form must be incessant; we cannot have peace. Let then our joy be in war; in uncompromising Action, which need not be the less a sagacious conduct of the war. . . . Action energizes men's brains, generates grander capacities, provokes greatness of soul between enemies, and is the guaranty of positive conquest for the benefit of our species.

THE brainless in Art and in State-craft are nothing but a little more obstructive than the dead. It is less easy to cut a way through them.

TRY to think individually upon what you have to learn collectively.

Do you know how the look of sunlight on a land calms one? It signifies to the eye possession and repose, the end gained, — not the end to labour, just heaven! but peace to the heart's craving,

which is the renewal of strength for work, the fresh
dip in the waters of life.

REMEMBER the meaning of Italian light and
colour; the clearness, the luminous fulness, the
thoughtful shadows. Mountain and wooded head-
land are solid, deep to the eye, spirit speaking to
the mind. They throb. You carve shapes of Gods
out of that sky, that sea, those peaks. They live
with you. How they satiate the vacant soul by
influx, and draw forth the troubled from its prickly
nest!

IN the presence of the irresistible, the conventional is a crazy structure, swept away with very
little creaking of its timbers on the flood.

THE carrying on of a prolonged and determined you-and-I in company intimates to those
undetermined floating atoms about us that a certain sacred something is in process of formation, or
has formed.

THE world is a variable monster; it rends the
weak, whether sincere or false; but those who weld

strength with sincerity may practise their rites of religion publicly, and it fawns to them and bellows to imitate.

STRENGTH in love is the sole sincerity.

IT is the soul which does things in life, — the rest is vapour.

LIGHT literature is the garden and the orchard, the fountain, the rainbow, the far view; the view within us, as well as without. Our blood runs through it, our history in the quick. The Philistine detests it, because he has no view, out or in. The dry confess they are cut off from the living tree, peeled and sapless, when they condemn it.

SHUN those who cry out against fiction, and despise it, and have no taste for elegant writing. Not to have a sympathy with the playful mind is not to have a mind.

YOU meet now and then men who have the woman in them without being womanized; they are the pick of men. And the choicest women are those who yield not a feather of their womanliness for some amount of manlike strength.

Who can hold her back when a woman is decided to move? Husbands have tried it vainly, and parents; and though the husband and the parent are not dealing with the same kind of woman, you see the same elemental power in her under both conditions of rebel wife and rebel daughter to break conventional laws and be splendidly irrational.

There is a nerve in brave warriors that does not like the battle before the crackle of musketry is heard and the big artillery.

The pusillanimous are under a necessity to be self-consoled when they are not self-justified; it is their instinctive manner of putting themselves in the right to themselves.

Accuracy of vision in our crises is not so uncommon as the proportionate equality of feeling: we do indeed frequently see with eyes of just measurement while we are conducting ourselves like madmen. The facts are seen, and yet the spinning nerves will change their complexion; and without enlarging or minimizing, they will alternate their effect on us immensely through the colour presenting them, — now sombre, now hopeful; doing its work of extravagance upon perceptibly plain matter.

WEAK souls are much moved by having the pathos on their side.

ALVAN was great-hearted; he could love in his giant fashion, love and lay down his life for the woman he loved, though the nature of the passion was not heavenly; or for the friend — who would have to excuse him often; or for the cause — which was to minister to his appetites. He was true man, a native of earth, and if he could not quit his huge personality to pipe spiritual music during a storm of trouble, being a soul wedged in the gnarled wood of the standing giant oak, and giving mighty sound of timber at strife rather than the angelical cry, he suffered, as he loved, to his depths.

Love and man sometimes meet for noble concord; the strings of the hungry instrument are not so rough that Love's touch on them is indistinguishable from the rattling of the wheel within; certain herald harmonies have been heard. But Love, which purifies and enlarges us and sets free the soul, Love visiting a fleshly frame, must have time and space, and some help of circumstances, to give the world assurance that the man is a temple fit for the rites.

At the age of forty, men that love, love rootedly. If the love is plucked from them, the life goes with it.

DIANA OF THE CROSSWAYS

DIANA OF THE CROSSWAYS.

WHAT a woman thinks of women is the test of her nature.

SMART remarks have their measured distances, many requiring to be *à brûle pourpoint*, or within throw of the pistol, to make it hit; in other words, the majority of them are addressed directly to our muscular system, and they have no effect when we stand beyond the range.

STILL, the promptness to laugh is an excellent progenitorial foundation for the wit to come in a people.

WHEN a nation has acknowledged that it is as yet but in the fisticuff stage of the art of condensing our purest sense to golden sentences, a readier appreciation will be extended to the gift, which is to strike, not the dazzled eyes, the unanticipating nose, the ribs, the sides, and stun us, twirl us, hoodwink, mystify, tickle, and twitch by dexterities of lingual sparrings and shufflings, but to strike roots in the mind, the Hesperides of good things.

IN England conversationally the men are the pointed talkers, and the women conversationally fair Circassians.

HE had by nature a tarnishing eye that cast discolouration.

NEVER should reputation of women trail a scent! How true! and true also that the women of waxwork never do; and that the women of happy marriages do not; nor the women of holy nunneries; nor the women lucky in their arts.

SHE told him that she read rapidly, "a great deal at one gulp," and thought in flashes,—a way with the maker of phrases.

"To be pointedly rational," she said, "is a greater difficulty to me than a fine delirium."

THE young who avoid the region [of Romance] escape the title of fool at the cost of a celestial crown.

THE sentimental people, in her phrase, fiddle harmonies on the strings of sensualism, — to the delight of a world gaping for marvels of musical execution rather than for music.

FOR our world is all but a sensational world at present, in maternal travail of a soberer, a braver, a brighter-eyed.

WE have to guard against "half-conceptions of wisdom, hysterical goodness, an impatient charity," against the elementary state of the altruistic virtues, distinguishable as the sickness and writhing of our egoism to cast its first slough.

SERVICE is our destiny in life or in death. Then let it be my choice living to serve the living and be fretted uncomplainingly. If I can assure myself of doing service, I have my home within.

To have the sense of the eternal in life is a short flight for the soul. To have had it is the soul's vitality.

PALLIATION of sin is the hunted creature's refuge and final temptation. Our battle is ever between spirit and flesh. Spirit must brand the flesh that it may live.

IN their judgments upon women, men are females, voices of the present (sexual) dilemma.

THEY [men] desire to have a still woman, who can make a constant society of her pins and needles. They create by stoppage a volcano, and are amazed at its eruptiveness.

OF the great loneliness of women she says, "It is due to the prescribed circumscription of their minds, of which they become aware in agitation. Were the walls about them beaten down, they would understand that solitariness is a common human fate, and the one chance of growth, like space for timber."

We are informed that the beginning of a motive life with women must be in the head equally with men. Also that men do not so much fear to lose the hearts of thoughtful women, as their strict attention to their graces.

DROLLERIES, humours, reputed witticisms, are like odors of roast meat, past with the pricking of the joint. Idea is the only vital breath.

HE gives good dinners, a candid old critic said, when asked how it was that he could praise a certain poet. In an island of chills and fogs, the comic and other perceptions are dependent on the stirrings of the gastric juices.

When our systems shall have been fortified by philosophy . . . then, ah! then, moreover, will the novelist's Art have attained its majority. We can then be veraciously historical, honestly transcriptive. Rose-pink and dirty drab will alike have passed away; Philosophy is the foe of both, and their silly cancelling contest perpetually renewed in a shuffle of extremes, as it always is where a phantasm falseness reigns, will no longer baffle the contemplation of natural flesh, smother no longer the soul issuing out of our incessant strife.

PHILOSOPHY bids us see that we are not so pretty as rose-pink, not so repulsive as dirty drab; and that, instead of everlastingly shifting those barren aspects, the sight of ourselves is wholesome, bearable, fructifying, finally a delight.

AND how may you know that you have reached to Philosophy? You touch her skirts when you share her hatred of the sham deceit, her derision of sentimentalism. You are one with her when — but I would not have you a thousand years older! Get to her, if in no other way, by the sentimental route, — that very winding path, which again and again brings you round to the point of original impetus, when you have to be unwound for another whirl; your point of original impetus being the grossly material, not at all the spiritual. It is most true that sentimentalism springs from the former, merely and badly aping the latter; fine flower or pinnacle flame-spire of sensualism that it is, could it do other?—and accompanying the former it traverses tracts of desert, here and there couching in a garden, catching in one hand at fruits, with another at colours; imagining a secret ahead, and goaded by an appetite sustained by sheer gratification. Fiddle in harmonies as it may, it will have these gratifications at all costs. Should none be discoverable, at once you are at the Cave of Despair, beneath the funereal orb of Glaucoma, in the thick midst of poniarded, slit-throat, rope-dependent figures, placarded across the bosom, Disillusioned, Infidel, Agnostic, Miserrimus. That is the sentimental route to advancement. Spirituality does not light it; evanescent dreams are its oil lamps, often with wick askant in the socket.

A THOUSAND years! You may count full many a thousand by this route before you are one with divine Philosophy. Whereas a single flight of brains will reach and embrace her; give you the savour of Truth, the right use of the senses, Reality's infinite sweetness; for these things are in Philosophy; and the fiction which is the summary of actual life, the within and without of us, is, prose or verse, plodding or soaring, Philosophy's elect handmaiden.

To such an end let us bend our aim to work, knowing that every form of labour, even the flimsiest, as you esteem it, should minister to growth. If in any branch of us we fail in growth, there is, you are aware, an unfailing aboriginal democratic old monster that waits to pull us down; certainly the branch, possibly the tree; and for the welfare of life we fall.

You are acutely conscious of yonder old monster when he is mouthing at you in politics. Be wary of him in the heart; especially be wary of the disrelish of brain-stuff. You must feed on something. Matter that is not nourishing to brains can help to constitute nothing but the bodies which are pitched on rubbish-heaps. Brain-stuff is not lean stuff; the brain-stuff of fiction is internal history, and to suppose it dull is the profoundest of errors: how deep you will understand when I tell you that it is the very football of the holiday afternoon imps below.

SURELY we owe a little to Time, to cheer his progress; a little to posterity and to our country. Dozens of writers will be in at yonder yawning breach if only perusers will rally to the philosophic standard. They are sick of the woodeny puppetry they dispense, as on a race-course, to the roaring frivolous.

A GREAT modern writer of clearest eye and head, now departed, capable in activity of presenting thoughtful women, thinking men, groaned over his puppetry, that he dared not animate them, flesh though they were, with the fires of positive brainstuff. He could have done it, and he is of the departed! Had he dared, he would (for he was Titan enough) have raised the Art in dignity on a level with History to an interest surpassing the narrative of public deeds as vividly as man's heart and brain in their union excel his plain lines of action to eruption.

INSTEAD, therefore, of objurgating the timid intrusions of Philosophy, invoke her presence, I pray you. History without her is the skeleton map of events, Fiction a picture of figures modelled on no skeleton anatomy. But each with Philosophy in aid blooms, and is humanly shapely. To demand of us truth to nature excluding Philosophy is really to bid a pumpkin caper. As much as legs are wanted for the dance, Philosophy is required to make our human nature credible and acceptable. Fiction implores you to have a bigger heart and take her in with this heavenly preservative helpmate, her inspiration and her essence.

THERE is a peep-show and a Punch's at the corner of every street, one magnifying the lacework of life, another the ventral tumulus, and it is these for you or dry bones if you do not open to philosophy.

BEAUTY is rare; luckily is it rare, or, judging from its effect on men, and the very strongest of them, our world would be internally a more distracted planet than we see, to the perversion of business, courtesy, rights of property, and the rest.

THE weather and women have some resemblance, they say. Is it true that he who reads one can read the other?

How odd it is that our men (Englishmen) show to such disadvantage in a ball-room. I have seen them in danger, and then they shine first of any, and one is proud of them. They should always be facing the elements or in action.

MEN are the barriers to perfect naturalness, at least with girls, I think.

THE burlesque Irishman can't be caricatured. Nature strained herself in a fit of absurdity to produce him, and all that Art can do is to copy.

IRISHMEN, as far as I have seen of them, are, like horses, bundles of nerves; and you must manage them, as you do with all nervous creatures, with firmness but good temper. You must never get into a fury of the nerves yourself with them. Spur and whip they don't want; they'll be off with you in a jiffy if you try it. They want the bridle rein. That seems to me the secret of the Irish character. We English are not bad horsemen. It's a wonder we blunder so in our management of such a people.

A WOMAN, Sir Lakin held, was by nature a mute in politics.

HE had neat phrases, opinions in packets. Beyond it, apparently, the world was void of any particular interest.

WHY she married him she never told. Possibly in amazement at herself subsequently she forgot the specific reason. That which weighs heavily in youth, and commits us to desperate action, will be a trifle under older eyes to blunter senses, a more enlightened understanding.

THERE were, one hears that there still are, remnants of the pristine male, who, if resisted in their suing, conclude that they are scorned, and it infuriates them; some also whose "passion for the charmer" is an instinct to pull down the standard of the sex, by a bully imposition of sheer physical ascendency, whenever they see it flying with an air of gallant independence; and some who dedicate their lives to a study of the arts of the Lord of Reptiles, until they have worked the crisis for a display of him in person.

SHE could not excuse her for having married the man. Her first and her final impression likened him to a house locked up and empty; a London house conventionally furnished and decorated by the upholsterer, and empty of inhabitants. . . . Empty of inhabitants even to the ghost! Both human and spiritual were wanting. The mind contemplating him became reflectively stagnant.

SHE [Diana] wrote this, which might have a secret personal signification: "We women are the verbs passive of the alliance, we have to learn, and if we take to activity with the best intentions, we conjugate a frightful disturbance. We are to run on lines, like the steam-trains, or we come to no station, dash to fragments. I have the misfortune to know I was born an active. I take my chance."

A WOMAN doubted by her husband is always, and even to her champions in the first hour of noxious rumour, until they have solidified in confidence through service, a creature of the wilds marked for our ancient running. Nay, more than a cynical world, these latter will be sensible of it. The doubt casts her forth, the general yelp drags her down; she runs like the prey of the forest under spotting branches; clear if we can think so, but it has to be thought in devotedness, her character is abroad.

THE world is ruthless, dear friends, because the world is hypocrite! The world cannot afford to be magnanimous.

SUCH are men in the world of facts, that when a woman steps out of her domestic tangle to assert because it is a tangle her rights to partial independence, they sight her as their prey, or at least they complacently suppose her accessible. Wretched at home, a woman ought to bury her wretchedness, else may she be assured that not the cleverest, wariest guard will cover her character.

THERE is perpetually the inducement to act the hypocrite before the hypocrite world, unless a woman submits to be the humbly knitting housewife, unquestioningly worshipful of her lord; for the world is all-gracious to an hypocrisy that pays homage to the mask of virtue by copying it, — the world hostile to the face of an innocence not conventionally simpering and quite surprised; the world prefers decorum to honesty.

ENGLISH women and men feel towards the quick-witted of their species as to aliens, having the demerits of aliens, — wordiness, vanity, obscurity, shallowness, an empty glitter, the sin of posturing. A quick-witted woman exerting her wit is both a foreigner and potentially a criminal.

OBSERVATION is one of the most enduring of the pleasures of life.

"YES, our lives require compression like romances to be interesting, and we object to the process," she said. "Real happiness is a state of dulness. When we taste it consciously it becomes mortal, — a thing of the seasons."

WHEN we have a man for arbiter, he is our sky.

THE world of a fluid civilization is perforce artificial.

IRISH anecdotes are always popular in England, as promoting besides the wholesome shake of the sides a kindly sense of superiority.

ANECDOTES also are portable, unlike the lightning flash, which will not go into the pocket; they can be carried home, they are disbursable at other tables. These were Diana's weapons. She discovered the social uses of cheap wit; she laid ambushes for anecdotes, a telling form of it among a people of no conversational interlocution, especially in the circles depending for dialogue upon perpetual fresh supplies of scandal; which have plentiful crops, yet not sufficient.

DOUBTLESS Cleopatra in her simple Egyptian uniform would hardly have won such plaudits as her stress of barbaric Oriental splendours evoked for her on the swan and serpent Nile-barge, — not from posterity at least. It is a terrible decree that all must act who would prevail; and the more extended the audience, the greater need for the mask and buskin.

WHEREVER Mrs. Warwick went, her arts of charming were addressed to the women. Men may be counted on for falling bowled over by a handsome face and pointed tongue; women require some wooing from their ensphered and charioted sister, particularly if she is clouded; and old women — excellent buttresses — must be suavely courted.

FEW tasks are more difficult than for a young woman under a cloud to hoodwink old women of the world. They are the prey of financiers; but Time has presented them a magic ancient glass to scan their sex in.

SHE was a lady of incisive features bound in stale parchment. Complexion she had none, but she had spotlessness of skin, and sons and daughters just resembling her, like cheaper editions of a precious quarto of a perished type.

HER appearance and her principles fitted her to stand for the Puritan rich of the period, emerging by the aid of an extending wealth into luxurious worldliness, and retaining the maxims of their forefathers for the discipline of the poor and erring.

THE upper class was gained by her intrepidity, her charm, and her elsewhere offending wit, however the case might go. It is chivalrous, but not, alas! inflammable in support of innocence. The class below it is governed in estimates of character by accepted patterns of conduct; yet where innocence under persecution is believed to exist, the members animated by that belief can be enthusiastic. Enthusiasm is a heaven-sent steeple-chaser, and takes a flying leap of the ordinary barriers; it is more intrusive than chivalry, and has a passion to communicate its ardour.

HE is not a contemptible man before the world; he is merely a very narrow one under close inspection. . . . Husband grew to mean to me stifler, lung contractor, iron mask, inquisitor, everything anti-natural. . . . He is an upright man; I have not seen marked meanness. One might build up a respectable figure in negatives. I could add a row of noughts to the single number he cherishes enough to make a millionaire of him; but strike away the first, the rest are wind. Which signifies that if you do not take his estimate of himself you will think little of his negative virtues. He is not eminently, that is to say, not saliently selfish; not rancorous, not obtrusive — ta-ta-ta. But dull! dull as a woollen night-cap over eyes and ears and mouth.

THE English notion of women seems to be that we are born white sheep or black; circumstances have nothing to do with our colour. They dread to grant distinctions, and to judge of us discerningly is beyond them. Whether the fiction that their homes are purer than elsewhere helps to establish the fact, I do not know; there is a class that do live honestly; and at any rate it springs from a liking for purity; but I am sure that their method of impressing it on women has the danger of things artificial. They narrow their understanding of human nature, and that is not the way to improve the breed.

"I SUPPOSE we women are taken to be the second thoughts of the Creator, human nature's fringes, mere finishing touches, not a part of the texture," said Diana, "the pretty ornamentation."

THE very young men and the old are our hope The middle-aged are hard and fast for existing facts. We pick *our* leaders on the slopes, the incline and decline of the mountains,—not on the upper table-land midway, where all appears to men so solid, so tolerably smooth, save for a few excrescences, roughnesses, gradually to be levelled at their leisure ; which induces one to protest that the middle-age of men is their time of delusion. It is no paradox. They may be publicly useful in a small way, I do not deny it at all. They must be near the gates of life — the opening or the closing — for their *minds* to be accessible to the urgency of the greater questions.

HE has a veritable thirst for hopeful views of the world, and no spiritual distillery of his own.

To be a girl again was magical. . . . And to be a girl with a woman's broader vision and receptive-

ness of soul, with knowledge of evil and winging to
ethereal happiness, this was a revelation of our
human powers.

WHEN a woman's charm has won half the battle,
her character is an advancing standard.

WE are much influenced in youth by sleepless
nights; they disarm, they predispose us to submit
to soft occasion; and in our youth occasion is
always coming.

PROSE can paint evening and moonlight, but
poets are needed to sing the dawn. That is
because prose is equal to melancholy stuff. Gladness requires the finer language.

WE have this power of resisting invasion of the
poetic by the commonplace, the spirit by the blood,
if we please, though you men may not think that
we have.

LONDON, say what we will of it, is after all the
head of the British giant, and if not the liveliest in

bubbles, it is past competition the largest broth-pot of brains anywhere simmering on the hob: over the steadiest of furnaces too. And the oceans and the continents, as you know, are perpetual and copious contributors, either to the heating apparatus or to the contents of the pot.

Let grander similes be sought. This one fits for the smoky receptacle cherishing millions magnetic to tens of millions more, with its caked outside of grime, and the inward substance incessantly kicking the lid, prankish but never casting it off. A good stew you perceive; not a parlous boiling. Weak as we may be in our domestic cookery, our political has been sagaciously adjusted as yet to catch the ardours of the furnace without being subject to their volcanic activities.

A WITTY woman is such salt that, where she has once been tasted, she must perforce be missed more than any of the absent, the dowering heavens not having yet showered her like very plentifully upon us.

LADY WATKINS's table could dispense with witty women, and for that matter witty men. The

intrusion of the spontaneous on the stereotyped
would have clashed. She preferred, as hostess,
the old legal anecdotes, sure of their laugh, and
the citations from the manufactories of fun in the
press, which were current and instantly intelligible
to all her guests.

THE more I know of the world, the more clearly
I perceive that its top and bottom sin is cowardice,
physically and morally alike. . . . We must fawn
in society. . . . Society is the best thing we have,
but it is a crazy vessel worked by a crew that for-
merly practised piracy, and now in expiation pro-
fesses piety, fearful of a discovered omnipotence
which is in the image of themselves and captain.

THERE was talk in the feminine world — at Lady
Watkins's assemblies. . . . Our aristocracy, brilliant
and ancient though it was, merited rebuke. She
grew severe upon aristocratic scandals, whereof
were plenty among the frolicsome host just overhead, as vexatious as the drawing-room party to
the lodger in the floor below, who has not received

an invitation to partake of the festivities, and is required to digest the noise.

But if ambition is over sensitive, moral indignation is ever consolatory, for it plants us on the judgment seat. There indeed we may, sitting with the very Highest, forget our personal disappointments in dispensing reprobation for misconduct, however eminent the offenders.

These book-worm women, whose pride it is to fancy that they can think for themselves, have a great deal of the heathen in them, as morality discovers when it wears the enlistment ribbons and applies to them to win recruits for a service under the direct blessing of Providence. . . . You sound them vainly for manifestation of the commonest human sensibilities. They turn over the leaves of a Latin book on their laps while you are supplicating them to assist in a work of charity.

August is the month of sober maturity and majestic foliage, songless, but a crowned and royal robed queenly month.

The Devil, he loudly proclaimed, has a multiplicity of lures, and none more deadly than when he baits with a petticoat.

Of Mrs. Warwick her opinion was formed. She would not have charged the individual creature with a criminal design; all she did was to stuff the person her virtue abhorred with all the wickedness of the world, and that is a common process in antipathy.

An astute world, right in the main, owing to perceptions based upon brute nature; utterly astray in particulars, for the reason that it takes no count of the soul of man or woman. Hence its glee at a catastrophe; its poor stock of mercy. And when no catastrophe follows, the prophet, for the honour of the profession, mus decry her as cunning beyond aught yet revealed of a serpent sex.

The world imagines those to be at our nature's depths who are imprudent enough to expose its muddy shallows. . . . "Exhibit humanity as it is wallowing, sensual, wicked, behind the mask," a voice called out to Diana; she was allured by the contemplation of the wide-mouthed old dragon Ego, whose portrait, decently painted, establishes an instant touch of exchange between author and public, the latter detected and confessing. Next to the pantomime of Humour and Pathos, a cynical surgical knife at the human bosom seems the surest talisman for this agreeable exchange.

Miss Paynham sketched on, with her thoughts in her bosom; a damsel castigatingly pursued by the idea of sex as the direct motive of every act of every person surrounding her; deductively, therefore, that a certain form of the impelling passion, mild or terrible or capricious, or it might be less pardonable, was unceasingly at work among the human couples up to decrepitude, — and she too frequently hit the fact to doubt her gift of reading into them.

Lady Pennon hinted "A good deal of what you so capitally call 'Green Tea talk' is going on, my dear." Diana replied without pretending to misunderstand. "Gossip is a beast of prey that does not wait for the death of the creature it devours."

We women miss life only when we have to confess we have never met the man to reverence.

The simplicity of the life of labour looked beautiful. What will not look beautiful contrasted with the fly in the web?

Gaze on the moral path you should have taken; you are asked for courage to commit a sanctioned suicide, by walking back to it stripped — a skeleton self.

When we are losing balance on a precipice we do not think much of the thing we have clutched for support. Our balance is restored and we have not fallen, — that is the comfortable reflection; we stand as others do, and we will for the future be warned to avoid the dizzy stations which cry for resources beyond a common equilibrium, and where a slip precipitates us to ruin.

They rose from table at ten, with the satisfaction of knowing that they had not argued, had not wrangled, had never stagnated, and were digestingly refreshed; as it should be among grown members of the civilized world, who mean to practise philosophy, making the hour of the feast a balanced recreation and a regeneration of body and mind.

A mind that after a long season of oblivion in pain returns to wakefulness without a keen edge for the world, is much in danger of souring permanently.

She would n't be a bad heroine of romance! He said it derisively of the Romantic. . . . Poor Diana was the flecked heroine of Reality; not always the same; not impeccable; not an ignorant innocent, nor a guileless; good under good leadings; devoted to the death in a grave crisis; often wrestling with her terrestrial nature nobly; and a growing soul; but not one whose purity was carved in marble for the assurance to an Englishman that his possession of the changeless thing defies time and his fellows,—is the pillow of his home and universally enviable.

Hymeneal rumours are those which might be backed to run a victorious race with the tale of evil future, and clearly for the reason that man's livelier half is ever alert to speed them. . . . Man's nuptial half is kindlingly concerned in the launch of a new couple; it is the business of the sex; and man himself lends a not unfavouring eye to the preparations of the matrimonial vessel for its oily descent into the tides, where billows will soon be rising, captain and mate soon discussing the fateful question of who is commander. We consent, it appears, to hope again for mankind; here is another chance! Or else, assuming the happiness of the pair, that pomp of ceremonial contrasted with the little wind-blown candle they carry between them catches at our weaker fibres. After so many ships have foundered, some keel up, like poisoned fish at the first drink of water, it is a gallant spectacle, let us avow; and either the world perpetuating it is heroical, or nature incorrigible in the species. Marriages are unceasing. Friends do it, and enemies; the unknown contractors of this engagement, or armistice, inspire an interest. It certainly is both exciting and comforting to hear that man and woman are ready to join in a mutual affirmative, say Yes together again. It sounds like the end of the war.

THEY who sow their money for a promising high percentage have built their habitations on the sides of the most eruptive mountain in Europe. Ætna supplies more certain harvests, wrecks fewer vineyards and peaceful dwellings.

WHO can really *think*, and not think hopefully? . . . When we despair or discolour things it is our senses in revolt, and they have made the sovereign brain their drudge. I hear you whisper with your very breath in my ear, "There is nothing the body suffers that the soul may not profit by." That is Emmy's history. With that I sail into the dark; it is my promise of the immortal; teaches me to *see* immortality for us.

True poets and true women have the native sense of the divineness of what the world deems gross material substance.

Men unaccustomed to a knot in their system find the project of cutting it an extreme relief, even when they know that the cut has an edge to wound mortally, as well as pacify.

The discussion closed with the accustomed pro and con upon the wart of Cromwell's nose, Realism rejoicing in it, Idealism objecting.

My vanity was my chief traitor. Cowardice of course played a part. In few things that we do where self is concerned will cowardice not be found.

When I think of it I perceive that Patience is our beneficent fairy godmother, who brings us our harvests in the long result.

Women who sap the moral laws pull down the pillars of the temple on their sex.

LET us stand aside and meditate on Life. If youth could only know, in the season of its reaping of pleasures, that it is but sowing doctor's bills.

ENTHUSIASM has the privilege of not knowing monotony.

THE HOUSE ON THE BEACH.

THE HOUSE ON THE BEACH.

How charged with language behind him is a dog! Everybody has noticed it. Let a dog turn away from a hostile circle, and his crisp and wavy tail not merely defends him, it menaces; it is a weapon. Man has no choice but to surge and boil or stiffen preposterously.

THE mixture of an idea of public duty with a feeling of personal rancour is a strong incentive to the pursuit of a stern line of conduct; and the glimmer of self-interest superadded does not check the steps of the moralist.

INFANTS are said to have their ideas, and why not young ladies? Those who write of their perplexities in descriptions comical in their length are unkind to them, by making them appear the simplest of the creatures of fiction; and most of us, I am sure, would incline to believe in them if they were only some bit more lightly touched. Those troubled sentiments of our young lady of the comfortable classes are quite worthy of mention. Her poor little eye, poring, as little fish-like as possible, upon the intricate, which she takes for the infinite, has its place in our history, nor would we any of us miss the pathos of it were it not that so large a space is claimed for the exposure.

ONE of the most difficult lessons for spirited young men to learn is, that good jokes are not always good policy. They have to be paid for, like good dinners, though dinner and joke shall seem to have been at some one else's expense.

VIGNETTES IN PROSE.

The art of the pen is to rouse the inward vision, instead of labouring with a drop scene brush, as if it were to the eye; because our flying minds cannot contain a protracted description. That is why the poets, who spring imagination with a word or a phrase, paint lasting pictures.

Nothing but poetry makes romances possible; for poetry is the everlastingly and embracingly human; without it, your fictions are flat foolishness.

VIGNETTES IN PROSE.

DAWN.

THE Adriatic was dark, the Alps had heaven to themselves. Crescents and hollows, rosy mounds, white shelves, shining ledges, domes and peaks, all the towering heights, were in illumination from Tivoli into farthest Tyrol; beyond earth to the stricken senses of the gazers. Colour was steadfast on the massive front ranks; it wavered in the remoteness, and was quick and dim as though it fell on beating wings: but there too divine colour seized and shaped forth solid forms, and thence away to others in uttermost distances where the incredible flickering gleam of new heights arose that soared, or stretched their white uncertain curves in sky, like wings traversing infinity.

Beauchamp's Career.

AFTER RAIN.

Rain had fallen in the night. Here and there hung a milk-white cloud with folded sail. The southwest left it its bay of blue, and breathed below. At moments the fresh scents of herb and mould swung richly in warmth. The young beech leaves glittered, pools of rain-water made the roadways laugh, the grass banks under hedges rolled their interwoven weeds in cascades of many-shaded green to right and left of the pair of dappled ponies, and a squirrel ahead, a lark went up a little way to ease his heart, closing his wings when the burst was over, startled blackbirds darting with a clamour like a broken cock-crow looped the wayside woods from hazel to oak-scrub ; short flights, quick spirits everywhere, steady sunshine above.

. . . .

February blew southwest for the pairing of the birds. A broad, warm wind rolled clouds of every ambiguity of form in magnitude over peeping azure, or skimming upon lakes of blue and lightest green, or piling the amphitheatre for majestic sunset, or sometimes those daughters of the wind flew linked and low, semi-purple, threatening the shower they retained, and teaching gloom to rouse a songful nest in the bosom of the viewer. Sometimes they were April, variable to soar with rain-skirts and sink with sun-shafts. Or they drenched wood and field for a day and opened on the high southwestern star. Daughters of the wind, but shifty daughters of this wind of the dropping suns, they have to be watched to be loved in their transformations.

. . . .

His elevation above the valley was about the knee-cap of Generoso. Waters of past rain-clouds poured down the mountain sides like veins of metal, here and there flinging off a shower on the busy descent; only dubiously animate in the lack-lustre of the huge bulk piled against a yellow east that wafted fleets of pinky cloudlets overhead. He mounted his path to a level with inviting grass-mounds where water circled, running from scoops and cups to curves and brook-streams, and in his fancy calling him to hear them.

. . . .

Heights to right and to left, and between them, aloft, a sky the rosy wheel-course of the chariot of morn, and below among the knolls choice of sheltered nook where waters whispered of secrecy to satisfy Diana herself. They have that whisper and waving of secrecy in secret scenery; they beckon to the bath; and they conjure classic visions of the pudency of the goddess, irate or unsighted.

Diana of the Crossways.

HER PICTURE.

SHE was indeed sweetly fair, and would have been held fair among rival damsels. On a magic shore, and to a youth educated by a system, strung like an arrow drawn to the head, he, it might be guessed, could fly fast and far with her. The soft rose in her cheeks, the clearness of her eyes, bore witness of the body's virtue and health and happy blood even in her bearing. The wide summer hat nodding over her forehead to her brows, seemed to flow with the flowing heavy curls, and those firethreaded mellow curls, only half-curls, waves of hair call them, rippling at the ends, went like a sunny red-veined torrent down her back almost to her

waist: a glorious vision to the youth who embraced it as a flower of beauty and read not a feature. There were curious features of colour in her face for him to have read. Her brows, thick and brownish against a soft skin showing the action of the blood, met in the bend of a bow, extending to the temples long and level; you saw that she was fashioned to peruse the sights of earth, and by the pliability of her brows that the wonderful creature used her faculty and was not going to be a statue to the gazer. Under the dark thick brows an arch of lashes shot out, giving a wealth of darkness to the full, frank blue eyes, a mystery of meaning — more than brain was ever meant to fathom: richer, therefore, than all mortal wisdom to Prince Ferdinand. For when Nature turns artist and produces contrasts of colours on a fair face, where is the Sage, or what the Oracle, shall match the depth of its lightest look?
The Ordeal of Richard Feverel.

TO-MORROW the place will have a memory, — the river, and the meadow, and the white falling weir:

his heart will build a temple here; and the skylark will be the high priest, and the old blackbird its glossy-gowned chorister, and there will be a sacred repast of dewberries. To-day the grass is grass; his heart is chased by phantoms and finds rest nowhere. Only when the most tender freshness of his flower comes across him does he taste a moment's calm; and no sooner does it come than it gives place to keen pangs of fear that she may not be his forever.

The Ordeal of Richard Feverel.

LOVE.

AWAY with systems! Away with a corrupt world! Let us breathe the air of the enchanted island. Golden lie the meadows; golden run the streams; red gold is on the pine stems. The sun is coming down to earth and walks the fields and the waters. The sun is coming down to earth, and the fields and the waters shoot to him golden shoots. He comes and his heralds run before him, and touch the leaves of oaks, and planes, and beeches lucid green, and the pine stems redder gold; leaving brightest footprints upon thickly-weeded banks, where the foxglove's last upper bells incline, and bramble shoots wander amid moist, rich herbage. The plumes of the woodland are alight; and beyond them, over the open, 't is a race with the long-thrown shadows; a race across the heaths and up the hills, till on the farthest bourne of mounted eastern cloud the heralds of the sun lay rosy fingers and rest.

Sweet are the shy recesses of the woodlands. The ray treads softly there. A film athwart the pathway quivers many-hued against purple shade fragrant with warm pines, deep moss-beds, feathery ferns. The little brown squirrel drops tail and leaps; the inmost bird is startled to a chance tuneless note. From silence into silence things move.

Peeps of the revelling splendour above and around enliven the conscious full heart within. The flaming west, the crimson heights, shower their glories through voluminous leafage. But these are bowers where deep bliss dwells, imperial joy, that owes no fealty to yonder glories, in which the young lamb gambols, and the spirits of men are glad. Descend, great Radiance! Embrace creation with beneficent fire and pass from us! You and the vice-regal light that succeeds to you, and all heavenly pageants, are the ministers and slaves of the throbbing contest within.

For this is the home of the enchantment. Here, secluded from vexed shores, the prince and princess of the island meet; here like darkling nightingales they sit, and into eyes and ears and hands pour endless ever-fresh treasures of their souls.

Roll on, grinding wheels of the world; cries of ships going down in a calm, groans of a system which will not know its rightful hour of exaltation, complain to the Universe. You are not heard here.

. . . .

Out in the world there, on the skirts of the woodland, a sheep-boy pipes to meditative eve on a penny whistle. Love's musical instrument is as old, and as poor: it has but two stops; and yet you see the cunning musician does this much with it!

Other speech they have little; light foam playing upon waves of feeling compact, that bursts only when the sweeping volume is too wild, and is no more than their sigh of tenderness spoken.

. . . .

Perhaps Love played his tune so well because their natures had unblunted edges, and were keen for bliss, confiding in it as natural food. To gentlemen and ladies, he fine-draws upon the viol ravishingly; or blows into the mellow bassoon; or rouses the heroic ardours of the trumpet; or it may be commands the whole orchestra for them. And they are pleased. He is still the cunning musician. They languish and taste ecstasy, but it is, however sonorous, an earthly concert. For them the spheres move not to two notes. They have lost or forfeited and never known the first supersensual spring of the ripe senses into passion; when they carry the soul with them, and have the privileges of spirits to walk disembodied, boundlessly to feel. Or one has it, and the other is a dead body. Ambrosia let them eat, and drink the nectar; here sit a couple to whom Love's simple bread and water is a finer feast.

Pipe, happy sheep-boy, Love! Irradiated angels, unfold your wings and lift your voices!

They have outflown Philosophy. Their instinct has shot beyond the ken of Science. They were made for their Eden.

They believe that the angels have been busy about them from their cradles. The celestial hosts have worthily striven to bring them together. And O victory! O wonder! after trial and pain, and difficulties exceeding, the celestial hosts have succeeded!

The Ordeal of Richard Feverel.

NATURE SPEAKS TO RICHARD FEVEREL.

THE moon was surpassingly bright; the summer air heavy and still. He left the high-road and pierced into the forest. His walk was rapid; the leaves on the trees brushed his cheeks; the dead leaves heaped in the dells noised to his feet.

. . . .

An oppressive slumber hung over the forest branches. In the dells and on the heights was the same dead heat. Here when the brook tinkled it was no cool-lipped sound, but metallic, and without the spirit of water. Yonder, in a space of moonlight on lush grass, the beams were as white fire to sight and feeling. No haze spread around. The valleys were clear, defined to the shadows of their verges; the distances sharply distinct, and with the colours of day but slightly softened. Richard beheld a roe moving across a slope of sward far out of rifle-mark. The breathless silence was significant, yet the moon shone in a broad blue heaven. Tongue out of mouth trotted the little dog after him; couched panting when he stopped an instant; rose weariedly when he started afresh. Now and then a large night-moth flitted through the dusk of the forest.

On a barren corner of the wooded highland looking inland stood gray topless ruins set in nettles and rank grass-blades. Richard mechanically sat down on the crumbling flints to rest, and listened to the panting of the dog. Sprinkled at his feet were emerald lights; hundreds of glow-worms studded the dark dry ground.

He sat and eyed them, thinking not at all. His energies were expended in action. He sat as a part of the ruins and the moon turned his shadow westward from the south. Overhead, as she declined, long ripples of silver cloud were imperceptibly stealing toward her. They were the van of a tempest. He did not observe them or the leaves beginning to chatter. When he again pursued his course with his face to the Rhine, a huge mountain appeared to rise sheer over him, and he had it in his mind to scale it. He got no nearer to the base of it for all his vigorous outstepping. The ground began to dip; he lost sight of the sky. Then heavy thunder-drops struck his cheek, the leaves were singing, the earth breathed, it was black before him and behind. All at once the thunder spoke. The mountain he had marked was bursting over him. Up started the whole forest in violet fire. He saw the country at the foot of the hills to the bounding Rhine gleam, quiver, extinguished. Then there were pauses; and the lightning seemed like the eye of heaven, and the thunder as the tongue of heaven, each alternately addressing him, filling him with awful rapture. Alone there—sole human creature among the grandeurs and mysteries of storm — he felt the representative of his kind, and his spirit rose, and marched, and exulted, let it be glory, let it be ruin! Lower down the lightened abysses of air rolled the wrathful crash; then white thrusts of light were darted from the sky, and great curving ferns, seen steadfast in pallor a second, were supernaturally agitated and vanished. Then a shrill song roused in the leaves and the herbage. Prolonged and louder it sounded, as deeper and heavier the deluge pressed. A mighty force of water satisfied the desire of the earth. Even in this, drenched as he was by the first outpouring, Richard had a savage pleasure. Keeping in motion, he was scarcely conscious of the wet, and the grateful breath of the weeds in his nostrils was refreshing. Suddenly he stopped short, lifting a curious nostril. He fancied he smelt meadow-sweet. He had never seen the flower in Rhineland,—never thought of it; and it could hardly be met with in a forest. He was sure he smelt it, fresh in dews. His little companion wagged a miserable wet tail some way in advance. He went on slowly, thinking indistinctly. After two or three steps he stooped and stretched out his hand to feel for the flower, having he knew not why a strong wish to verify its growth there. Groping about, his hand encountered something warm that started at the touch, and he, with the instinct we have, seized it and lifted it to look at it. The creature was very small, evidently quite young. Richard's eyes, now accustomed to the darkness, were able to discern it for what it was, a tiny leveret, and he supposed that the dog had probably frightened its dam just before he found it. He put the little thing on one hand in his breast and stepped out rapidly as before.

The rain was now steady: from every tree a fountain poured. So cool and easy had his mind become that he was speculating on what kind of shelter the birds could find, and how the butterflies and moths saved their coloured wings from washing. Folded close, they might hang under a leaf, he thought. Lovingly he looked into the dripping darkness of the coverts on each side, as one of their children. Then he was musing on a strange sensation he experienced. It ran up one arm with an indescribable thrill, but communicated nothing to his heart. It was purely physical, ceased for a time, and recommenced, till he had it all through his blood wonderfully thrilling. He grew aware that the little thing he carried in his breast was licking his hand there. The small rough tongue going over and over the palm of his hand produced this strange sensation he felt. Now that he knew the cause, the marvel ended; but now that he knew the cause, his heart was touched, and made more of it. The gentle scraping continued without intermission as on he walked. What did it say to him? Human tongue could not have said so much then.

A pale gray light on the skirts of the flying tempest displayed the dawn. Richard was walking hurriedly. The green drenched weeds lay about in his path, bent thick, and the forest drooped glimmeringly. Impelled as a man who feels a revelation mounting obscurely to his brain, Richard was passing one of those little forest chapels hung with votive wreaths, where the peasant halts to kneel and pray. Cold, still, in the twilight it stood, raindrops pattering round it. He looked within, and saw the Virgin holding her Child. He moved by. But not many steps had he gone ere his strength was out of him, and he shuddered.

What was it? He asked not. He was in other

hands. Vivid as lightning the spirit of Life illumined him. He felt in his heart the cry of his child, his darling's touch. With shut eyes he saw them both. They drew him from the depths; they led him, a blind and tottering man. And as they led him, he had a sense of purification so sweet he shuddered again and again.

When he looked out from his trance on the breathing world, the small birds hopped and chirped; warm fresh sunlight was over all the hills. He was on the edge of the forest, entering a plain clothed with ripe corn under a spacious morning sky.

The Ordeal of Richard Feverel.

SONNETS.

"An inspiration caught from dubious hues
  Filled him, and mystic wrynesses he chased."

SONNETS.

MY THEME.

OF me and of my theme think what thou wilt:
The song of gladness one straight bolt can check.
But I have never stood at Fortune's beck:
Were she and her light crew to run atilt
At my poor holding, little would be spilt;
Small were the praise for singing o'er that wreck.
Who courts her dooms to strife his bended neck;
He grasps a blade, not always by the hilt.
Nathless she strikes at random, can be fell
With other than those votaries she deals
The black or brilliant from her thunder-rift.
I say but that this love of Earth reveals
A soul beside our own to quicken, quell,
Irradiate, and through ruinous floods uplift.

THE WORLD'S ADVANCE.

Judge mildly the tasked world; and disincline
To brand it, for it bears a heavy pack.
You have perchance observed the inebriate's track
At night when he has quitted the inn-sign:
He plays diversions on the homeward line,
Still that way bent albeit his legs are slack:
A hedge may take him, but he turns not back,
Nor turns this burdened world, of curving spine.
"Spiral," the memorable Lady terms
Our mind's ascent: our world's advance presents
That figure on a flat; the way of worms.
Cherish the promise of its good intents,
And warn it, not one instinct to efface
Ere Reason ripens for the vacant place.

THE DISCIPLINE OF WISDOM.

Rich labour is the struggle to be wise,
While we make sure the struggle cannot cease.
Else better were it in some bower of peace
Slothful to swing, contending with the flies.

You point at Wisdom fixed on lofty skies,
As mid barbarian hordes a sculptured Greece :
She falls. To live and shine, she grows her fleece,
Is shorn, and rubs with follies and with lies.
So following her, your hewing may attain
The right to speak unto the mute, and shun
That sly temptation of the illumined brain,
Deliveries oracular, self-spun.
Who sweats not with the flock will seek in vain
To shed the words which are ripe fruit of sun.

APPRECIATION.

EARTH was not earth before her sons appeared,
Nor Beauty Beauty ere young Love was born :
And thou when I lay hidden wert as morn
At city windows, touching eyelids bleared ;
To none by her fresh wingedness endeared ;
Unwelcome unto revellers outworn.
I the last echoes of Diana's horn
In woodland heard, and saw thee come, and
    cheered.
No longer wert thou then mere light, fair soul !

And more than simple duty moved thy feet.
New colours rose in thee, from fear, from shame,
From hope, effused: though not less pure a scroll
May men read on the heart I taught to beat:
That change in thee, if not thyself, I claim.

EARTH'S SECRET.

Not solitarily in fields we find
Earth's secret open, though one page is there;
Her plainest, such as children spell, and share
With bird and beast; raised letters for the blind.
Not where the troubled passions toss the mind,
In turbid cities, can the key be bare.
It hangs for those who hither thither fare,
Close interthreading nature with our kind.
They, hearing History speak, of what men were,
And have become, are wise. The gain is great
In vision and solidity; it lives.
Yet at a thought of life apart from her,
Solidity and vision lose their state,
For Earth, that gives the milk, the spirit gives.

SENSE AND SPIRIT.

The senses loving Earth or well or ill,
Ravel yet more the riddle of our lot.
The mind is in their trammels, and lights not
By trimming fear-bred tales; nor does the will
To find in nature things which less may chill
An ardour that desires, unknowing what.
Till we conceive her living we go distraught,
At best but circle-windsails of a mill.
Seeing she lives, and of her joy of life
Creatively has given us blood and breath
For endless war and never wound unhealed,
The gloomy Wherefore of our battle-field
Solves in the Spirit, wrought of her through strife
To read her own and trust her down to death.

POEMS.

POEMS.

LOVE IN THE VALLEY.

UNDER yonder beech tree single on the green-
    sward,
Couched with her arms behind her golden head,
Knees and tresses folded to slip and ripple idly,
Lies my young love sleeping in the shade.
Had I the heart to slide an arm beneath her,
Press her parting lips as her waist I gather slow,
Waking in amazement she could not but embrace
    me;
Then would she hold me and never let me go?

   .   .   .   .

Shy as the squirrel and wayward as the swallow,
Swift as the swallow along the river's light
Circleting the surface to meet his mirrored wing-
    lets,
Fleeter she seems in her stay than in her flight;

Shy as the squirrel that leaps among the pine-tops,
Wayward as the swallow overhead at set of sun,
She whom I love is hard to catch and conquer, —
Hard, but O the glory of the winning were she won !

. . . .

When at dawn she sighs, and like an infant to the window
Turns grave eyes craving light, released from dreams,
Beautiful she looks, like a white water-lily
Bursting out of bed in havens of the streams.
When from bed she rises clothed from neck to ankle
In her long night-gown sweet as boughs of May,
Beautiful she looks, like a tall garden lily
Pure from the night, and splendid for the day.

. . . .

Doves of the fir-wood walling high our red roof
Thro' the long noon coo, crooning thro' the coo,
Loose droop the leaves, and down the sleepy roadway
Sometimes pipes a chaffinch; loose droops the blue.

Cows flap a slow tail knee-deep in the river,
Breathless, given up to sun and gnat and fly:
Nowhere is she seen; and if I see her nowhere,
Lightning may come, straight rains, and tiger sky.

．　　．　．ˊ　．　　．　　．　　．

Soft new beech-leaves, up to beamy April
Spreading bough on bough a primrose mountain, you,
Lucid in the moon, raise lilies to the sky-fields,
Youngest green transfused in silver shining through;
Fairer than the lily, than the wild white cherry, —
Fair as in image my seraph love appears,
Borne to me by dreams when dawn is at my eyelids,
Fair as in the flesh she swims to me on tears.

．　．　．　．　．　．　．

Could I find a place to be alone with heaven,
I would speak my heart out; heaven is my need.
Every woodland tree is flushing like the dogwood,
Flashing like the whitebeam, swaying like the reed;
Flushing like the dogwood crimson in October,
Streaming like the flag-reed southwest blown,
Flashing as in gusts the sudden-lighted whitebeam,
All seem to know what is for heaven alone.

FRANCE. — DECEMBER, 1870.

I.

We look for her that sunlike stood
Upon the forehead of our day,
An orb of nations, radiating food
For body and for mind alway;
Where is the shape of glad array;
The nervous hands, the front of steel,
The clarion tongue? Where is the bold, proud face?
    We see a vacant place,
    We hear an iron heel.

II.

O she that made the brave appeal
For manhood when our time was dark,
And from our fetters drove the spark
Which was as lightning to reveal
New seasons, with the swifter play
Of pulses, and benigner day, —
She that divinely shook the dead
From living man, that stretched ahead
Her resolute forefinger straight,
And marched toward the gloomy gate

Of earth's Untried, gave note, and in
The good name of Humanity
Called forth the daring vision! She,
She likewise half-corrupt of sin,
Angel and Wanton! Can it be?
Her star has foundered in eclipse,
The shriek of madness on her lips;
Shreds of her, and no more, we see.
There is horrible convulsion, smothered din,
As of one that in a grave-cloth struggles to be free!

III.

Look not for spreading boughs
On the riven forest tree,
Look down where deep in blood and mire
Black thunder plants his feet and ploughs
The soil for ruin; that is France;
Still thrilling like a lyre,
Amazed to shivering discord from a fall
Sudden as that the lurid hosts recall
Who met in heaven the irreparable mischance,
  O, that is France!
The brilliant eyes to kindle bliss,
The shrewd quick lips to laugh and kiss,

Breasts that a sighing world inspire,
And laughter-dimpled countenance,
Where soul and senses caught desire!

IV.

Ever invoking fire from Heaven, the fire
Has grasped her, unconsumable, but framed
For all the ecstasies of suffering dire :
Mother of Pride, her sanctuary shamed :
Mother of Delicacy, and made a mark
For outrage ; Mother of Luxury stripped stark :
Mother of Heroes, bondsmen : thro' the rains,
Across her boundaries, lo the league-long chains !
Fond Mother of her martial youth ; they pass,
Are spectres in her sight, are mown as grass !
Mother of Honour, and dishonoured : Mother
Of Glory, she condemned to crown with bays
Her victor, and be fountain of his praise.
Is there another curse? There is another.
Compassionate her madness ; is she not
Mother of Reason? she that sees them mown
Like grass, her young ones ! Yea, in the low groan
And under the fixed thunder of this hour
Which holds the animate world in one foul blot

Tranced circumambient, while relentless Power
Beaks at her heart and claws her limbs down-
    thrown,
She, with the plunging lightnings overshot,
With madness for an armour against pain,
With milkless breasts for little ones athirst,
And round her all her noblest dying in vain,
Mother of Reason is she, trebly cursed,
To feel, to see, to justify the blow ;
Chamber to chamber of her sequent brain
Gives answer to the cause of her great woe,
Inexorably echoing thro' the vaults,
" 'T is thus they reap in blood, in blood who sow :
This is the sum of self-absolvéd faults."
Doubt not that thro' her grief, with sight supreme,
Thro' her delirium and despair's last dream,
Thro' pride, thro' bright illusion, and the brood
Bewildering of her various Motherhood,
The high strong life within her, tho' she bleeds,
Traces the letters of returned misdeeds.
She sees what seed long sown, ripened of late,
Bears this fierce crop ; and she discerns her fate
From origin to agony, and on
As far as the wave washes long and wan

Off one disastrous impulse : for of waves
Our life is, and our deeds are pregnant graves
Blown rolling to the sunset from the dawn.

V.

Ah, what a dawn of splendour, when her sowers
Went forth and bent the necks of populations,
And of their terrors and humiliations
Wove her the starry wreath that earthward lowers
Now in the figure of a burning yoke!
Her legions traversed North and South and East,
Of triumph they enjoyed the glutton's feast:
They grafted the green sprig, they lopped the oak,
They caught by the beard the tempests, by the scalp
The icy precipices, and clove sheer through
The heart of horror of the pinnacled Alp,
Emerging not as men whom mortals knew.
They were the earthquake and the hurricane,
The lightnings and the locusts, plagues of blight,
Plagues of the revel: they were Deluge rain,
And dreaded Conflagration, lawless might.
Death writes a reeling line along the snows,
Where under frozen mists they may be tracked,
Who men and elements provoked to foes,

And Gods: they were of God and Beast compact:
Abhorred of all. Yet how they sucked the teats
Of Carnage, thirsty issue of their dam,
Whose eagles, angrier than their oriflamme,
Flushed the vext earth with blood, green earth
    forgets.
The gay young generations mask her grief;
Where bled her children hangs the loaded sheaf.
Forgetful is green earth; the Gods alone
Remember everlastingly: they strike
Remorselessly, and ever like for like,
By their great memories the Gods are known.

VI.

They are with her now, and in her ears, and known.
'T is they that cast her to the dust for Strength,
Their slave, to feed on her fair body's length,
That once the sweetest and the proudest shone;
Scoring for hideous dismemberment
Her limbs, as were the anguish-taking breath
Gone out of her in the insufferable descent
From her high chieftainship; as were she death
Who hears a voice of Justice, feels the knife
Of torture, drinks all ignominy of life.

They are with her, and the painful Gods might weep,
If ever rain of tears came out of heaven
To flatter Weakness and bid Conscience sleep,
Viewing the woe of this Immortal, driven
For the soul's life to drain the maddening cup
Of her own children's blood implacably:
Unsparing even as they to furrow up
The yellow land to likeness of a sea:
The bountiful fair land of vine and grain,
Of wit and grace and ardour, and strong roots,
Fruits perishable, imperishable fruits;
Furrowed to likeness of the dim gray main
Behind the black obliterating cyclone.

VII.

Behold, the Gods are with her, and are known.
Whom they abandon misery persecutes
No more: them half-eyed apathy may loan
The happiness of pitiable brutes.
Whom the just Gods abandon have no light,
No ruthless light of introspective eyes
That in the midst of misery scrutinize
The heart and its iniquities outright.

They rest, they smile and rest; have earned perchance
Of ancient service quiet for a term;
Quiet of old men dropping to the worm;
And so goes out the soul.   But not of France.
She cries for grief, and to the Gods she cries,
For fearfully their loosened hands chastize,
And icily they watch the rod's caress
Ravage her flesh from scourges merciless,
But she, inveterate of brain, discerns
That Pity has as little place as Joy
Among their roll of gifts; for Strength she yearns,
For Strength, her idol once, too long her toy.
Lo, Strength is of the plain root Virtues born:
Strength shall ye gain by service, prove in scorn,
Train by endurance, by devotion shape.
Strength is not won by miracle or rape.
It is the offspring of the modest years,
The gift of sire to son, thro' those firm laws
Which we name Gods; which are the righteous cause,
The cause of man, and manhood's ministers.
Could France accept the fables of her priests,
Who blest her banners in this game of beasts,

And now bid hope that Heaven will intercede
To violate its laws in her sore need,
She would find comfort in their opiates:
Mother of Reason! Can she cheat the Fates?
Would she, the champion of the open mind,
The Omnipotent's prime gift,—the gift of growth,—
Consent even for a night-time to be blind,
And sink her soul on the delusive sloth,
For fruits ethereal and material, both,
In peril of her place among mankind?
The Mother of the many Laughters might
Call one poor shade of laughter in the light
Of her unwavering lamp, to mark what things
The world puts faith in, careless of the truth:
What silly puppet-bodies danced on strings,
Attached by credence, we appear in sooth,
Demanding intercession, direct aid,
When the whole tragic tale hangs on a broken blade!

She swung the sword for centuries; in a day
It slipped her, like a stream cut off from source.
She struck a feeble hand, and tried to pray,
Clamoured of treachery, and had recourse
To drunken outcries in her dream that Force

Needed but hear her shouting to obey.
Was she not formed to conquer? The bright
    plumes
Of crested vanity shed graceful nods :
Transcendent in her foundries, Arts, and looms,
Had France to fear the vengeance of the Gods?
Her faith was on her battle-roll of names
Sheathed in the records of old war ; with dance
And song she thrilled her warriors and her dames,
Embracing her Dishonourer ; gave him France
From head to foot, France present and to come,
So she might hear the trumpet and the drum —
Bellona and Bacchante ! — rushing forth
On yon stout marching Schoolmen of the North.

Inveterate of brain, well knows she why
Strength failed her, faithful to himself the first :
Her dream is done, and she can read the sky,
And she can take into her heart the worst
Calamity to drug the shameful thought
Of days that made her as the man she served,
A name of terror, but a thing unnerved :
Buying the trickster, by the trickster bought,
She for dominion, he to patch a throne.

VIII.

Henceforth of her the Gods are known,
Open to them her breast is laid.
Inveterate of brain, heart valiant,
Never did fairer creature pant
Before the altar and the blade!

IX.

Swift fall the blows, and men upraid,
And friends give echo blunt and cold,
The echo of the forest to the axe
Within her are the fires that wax
For resurrection from the mould.

X.

She snatched at heaven's flame of old,
And kindled nations: she was weak:
Frail sister of her heroic prototype,
The man; for sacrifice unripe,
She too must fill a Vulture's beak,
Deride the vanquished, and acclaim
The conqueror, who stains her fame.
Still the Gods love her, for that of high aim
Is this good France, the bleeding thing they stripe.

XI

She shall rise worthier of her prototype
Thro' her abasement deep: the pain that runs
From nerve to nerve some victory achieves.
They lie like circle-strewn soaked Autumn leaves
Which stain the forest scarlet, her fair sons!
And of their death her life is: of their blood
From many streams now urging to a flood,
No more divided, France shall rise afresh.
Of them she learns the lesson of the flesh, —
The lesson writ in red since first Time ran
A hunter hunting down the beast in man:
That till the chasing out of its last vice,
The Flesh were fashioned but for sacrifice.

Immortal Mother of a mortal host!
Thou suffering of the wounds that will not slay,
Wounds that bring death but take not life away!
Stand fast and hearken while thy victors boast,
Hearken, and loathe that music evermore!
Slip loose thy garments woven of pride and shame;
The torture lurks in them, with them the blame

Shall pass to leave thee purer than before;
Undo thy jewels, thinking whence they came,
For what, and of the abominable name
Of her who in imperial beauty wore.

O Mother of a fated fleeting host
Conceived in the past days of sin, and born
Heirs of disease and arrogance and scorn,
Surrender, yield the weight of thy great ghost,
Like wings on air, to what the heavens proclaim
With trumpets from the multitudinous mounds
Where peace has filled the hearing of thy sons:
Albeit a pang of dissolution rounds
Each new discernment of the undying ones,
Do thou stoop to these graves here scattered wide
Along thy fields, as sunless billows roll;
These ashes have the lesson for the soul.
" Die to thy Vanity, and strain thy Pride,
Strip off thy Luxury; that thou may'st live
Die to thyself," they say, " as we have died
From dear existence, and the foe forgive,
Nor pray for aught save in our little space
To warm good seed to greet the fair Earth's face."
O Mother! take their counsel, and so shall

The broader world breathe in on this thy home,
Light clear for thee the counter-changing dome,
Strength give thee, like an ocean's vast expanse
Off mountain cliffs, the generations all,
Not whirling in their narrow rings of foam,
But as a river forward.   Soaring France !
Now is Humanity on trial in thee :
Now may'st thou gather human kind in fee :
Now prove that Reason is a quenchless scroll ;
Make of calamity thine aureole,
And bleeding lead us thro' the troubles of the sea.

MEN AND MAN.

I.

MEN the Angels eyed ;
And here they were wild waves,
And there as marsh descried.
Men the Angels eyed,
And liked the picture best
Where they were greenly dressed
In brotherhood of graves.

II.

Man the Angels marked:
He led a host through murk,
On fearful seas embarked,
Man the Angels marked;
To think without a nay,
That he was good as they,
And help him at his work.

III.

Man and Angels, ye
A sluggish fen shall drain,
Shall quell a warring see.
Man and Angels, ye,
Whom stain of strife befouls,
A light to kindle souls
Bear radiant in the stain.

THE WOODS OF WESTERMAIN.

Enter these enchanted woods,
    You who dare.
Nothing harms beneath the leaves
More than waves a swimmer cleaves.

Toss your heart up with the lark,
Foot at peace with mouse and worm,
    Fair yon fare
Only at a dread of dark
Quaver, and they quit their form :
Thousand eyeballs under hoods
Have you by the hair.
Enter these enchanted woods,
    You who dare.

    .   .   .   .   .   .

On the surface she will witch,
Rendering Beauty yours, but gaze
Under, and the soul is rich
Past computing, past amaze.
Then is courage that endures
Even her awful tremble yours.
Then, the reflex of that Fount
Spied below, with Reason mount
Lordly and a quenchless force,
Lighting Pain to its mad source,
Scaring Fear till Fear escapes,
Shot through all its phantom shapes.
Then your spirit will perceive
Fleshly seed of fleshly sins ;

When the passions interweave,
How the serpent tangle spins
Of the sense of Earth misprised
Brainlessly unrecognized;
She being Spirit in her clods,
Footway to the God of Gods.
Then for you are pleasures pure,
Sureties as the stars are sure:
Not the wanton beckoning flags
Which, of flattery and delight,
Wag to the grim Habit-Hags
Riding souls of men to night;
Pleasures that through blood run sane,
Quickening spirit from the brain.
Each of each in sequent birth,
Blood and brain and spirit, three
(Say the deepest gnomes of Earth)
Join for true felicity.
Are they parted, then expect
Some one sailing will be wrecked.

. . . .

THE LARK ASCENDING.

He rises and begins to round,
He drops the silver chain of sound
Of many links without a break
In chirrup, whistle, slur, and shake,
All intervolved, and spreading wide,
Like water-dimples down a tide,
Where ripple ripple overcurls
And eddy into eddy whirls.

. . . .

For, singing till his heaven fills,
'T is love of earth that he instils,
And ever winging up and up
Our valley is his golden cup,
And he the wine which overflows
To lift us with him as he goes:
The woods and brooks, the sheep and kine,
He is, the hills, the human line,
The meadows green, the fallows brown,
The dreams of labour in the town;
He sings the sap, the quickened veins,
The wedding song of sun and rains

He is, the dance of children, thanks
Of sowers, shoot of primrose banks,
And eye of violets while they breathe;
All these the circling song will wreathe,
And you shall hear the herb and tree,
The better heart of men shall see,
Shall feel celestially, as long
As you crave nothing save the song.

Was never voice of ours could say
Our inmost in the sweetest way
Like yonder voice aloft, and link
All hearers in the song they drink;
Our wisdom speaks from failing blood,
Our passion is too full in flood,
We want the key of his wild note
Of truthful in a tuneful throat,
The song seraphically free
Of taint of personality,
So pure that it salutes the suns,
The voice of one for millions
In whom the millions rejoice
For giving them one spirit voice.

AUTUMN EVEN-SONG

THE long cloud edged with streaming gray,
    Soars from the west;
The red leaf mounts with it away,
    Showing the nest
A blot among the branches bare:
There is a cry of outcasts in the air.

Swift little breezes, darting chill,
    Part down the lake;
A crow flies from the yellow hill,
    And in its wake
A baffled line of labouring rooks;
Steel-surfaced to the light the river looks.

. . . .

Pale the rain-rutted roadways shine
    In the green light,
Behind the cedar and the pine:
    Come, thundering night!
Blacken broad earth with hoards of storm!
For me yon valley-cottage beckons warm.

BY THE ROSANNA.

To F. M.

Stanza-Thal, Tyrol.

THE old gray Alp has caught the cloud
And the torrent river sings aloud;
The glacier-green Rosanna sings
An organ song of its upper springs,
Foaming under the tiers of pine.
I see it dash down the dark ravine,
And it tumbles the rocks in boisterous play,
With an earnest will to find its way.

. . . .

A chain of foam from end to end,
And a solitude so deep, my friend,
You may forget that man abides
Beyond the great mute mountain-sides.
Yet to me, in this high-walled solitude
Of river and rock and forest rude,
The roaring voice through the long white chain
Is the voice of the world of bubble and brain.

I find it when I sought it least;
I sought the mountain and the beast,

The young thin air that knits the nerves,
The chamois ledge, the snowy curves ;
Earth in her whiteness looking bold
To Heaven forever as of old.

And lo, if I translate the sound
Now thundering in my ears around
'T is London rushing down a hill :
Life or London, — which you will !

. . . .

ODE

To the Spirit of Earth in Autumn.

FAIR mother Earth lay on her back last night
To gaze her fill on Autumn's sunset skies,
When at a waning of the fallen light
Sprang realms of rosy fruitage o'er her eyes.
A lustrous heavenly orchard hung the West,
Wherein the blood of Eden bloomed again ;
Red were the myriad cherub mouths that pressed
Among the clusters, rich with song, full fain,
But dumb, because that overmastering spell
Of rapture held them dumb, then, here and there,

A golden harp lost strings ; a crimson shell
Burnt gray ; and sheaves of lustre fell to air.
The illimitable eagerness of hue
Bronzed, and the beamy winged bloom that flew
Mid those bunched fruits and thronging figures failed.
A green-edged lake of saffron touched the blue
With isles of fireless purple lying through,
And Fancy on that lake to seek lost treasures sailed.

Not long the silence followed
The voice that issues from thy breast,
O glorious South-West,
Along the gloom-horizon holloa'd,
Warning the valleys with a mellow roar
Thro' flapping wings ; then sharp the woodland bore
A shudder, and a noise of hands ;
A thousand horns from some far vale
In ambush sounding on the gale.
Forth from the cloven sky came bands
Of revel-gathering spirits ; trooping down,
Some rode the tree-tops ; some on torn cloud-strips
Burst screaming thro' the lighted town :
And scudding seaward, some fell on big ships,
Or mounting the sea-horses blew

Bright foam-flakes on the black review
Of heaving hulls and burying beaks.

. . . .

Night on the rolling foliage fell!
But I, who love old hymning night,
And know the Dryad voices well,
Discerned them as their leaves took flight,
Like souls to wander after death:
Great armies in imperial dyes,
And mad to tread the air, and rise,
The savage freedom of the skies
To taste before they rot. And here,
Like frail white-bodied girls in fear,
The birches swung from shrieks to sighs;
The aspens, laughers at a breath,
In showering spray-falls mixed their cries,
Or raked a savage ocean-strand
With one incessant drowning screech.
Here stood a solitary beech,
That gave its gold with open hand
And all its branches, toning chill,
Did seem to shut their teeth right fast,
To shriek more mercilessly shrill
And match the fierceness of the blast.

. . . . . .

Oh, mother Nature! teach me, like thee,
To kiss the season, and shun regrets.
And am I more than the mother who bore,
Mock me not with thy harmony!
Teach me to blot regrets,
Great Mother! me inspire
With faith that forward sets
But feeds the living fire,
Faith that never frets
For vagueness in the form.
In life, O keep me warm!
For what is human grief?
And what do men desire?
Teach me to feel myself the tree,
And not the withered leaf,
Fixed am I, and await the dark to be!

And O, green bounteous earth!
Bacchante Mother! stern to those
Who live not in thy heart of mirth;
Death shall I shrink from, loving thee?
Into the breast that gives the rose,
Shall I with shuddering fall?

Earth, the mother of all,
Moves on her steadfast way,
Gathering, flinging, sowing.
Mortals, we live in her day,
She in her children is growing.

She can lead us, only she,
Unto God's footstool, whither she reaches :
Loved, enjoyed, her gifts must be ;
Reverenced the truths she teaches,
Ere a man may hope that he
Ever can attain the glee
Of things without a destiny !

.   .   .   .

And may not men to this attain?
That the joy of motion, the rapture of being,
Shall throw strong light when their season is fleeing,
Nor quicken aged blood in vain,
At the gates of the vault, on the verge of the plain?
Life thoroughly lived is a fact in the brain,
While eyes are left for seeing.

Behold, in yon stripped Autumn, shivering gray,
Earth knows no desolation,

She smells regeneration
In the moist breath of decay.

Prophetic of the coming joy and strife,
Like the wild western war-chief sinking
Calm to the end he eyes unblinking,
Her voice is jubilant in ebbing life.

SPRING.

. . . .

The day was a van-bird of summer; the robin still piped, but the blue,
A warm and dreamy palace with voices of larks ringing through,
Looked down as if wistfully eying the blossoms that fell from its lap;
A day to sweeten the juices, — a day to quicken the sap!
All round the shadowy orchard sloped meadows in gold, and the dear
Shy violets breathed their hearts out, — the maiden breath of the year!

Grandfather Bridgeman.

MODERN LOVE.

. . . .

She issues radiant from her dressing-room
Like one prepared to scale an upper sphere
By stirring up a lower, much I fear!
How deftly that oiled barber lays his bloom!
That long-shanked dapper Cupid with frisked curls
Can make known women torturingly fair;
The gold-eyed serpent dwelling in rich hair
Awakes beneath his magic whisks and twirls.
His art can take the eyes from out my head
Until I see with eyes of other men.

. . . .

Out in the yellow meadows, when the bee
Hums by us with the honey of the spring,
And showers of sweet notes from the larks on wing
Are dropping like a noon-dew, wander we.
Or is it now? Or was it then? For now,
As then, the larks from running rings send showers;
The golden foot of May is on the flowers,
And friendly shadows dance upon her brow.
What's this, when Nature swears there is no change
To challenge eyesight? Now, as then, the grace

Of Heaven seems holding Earth in its embrace,
Nor eyes, nor heart as she to feel it strange?

. . . .

" I play for Seasons; not Eternities!"
Says Nature, laughing on her way. "So must
All those whose stake is nothing more than
 dust!"
And lo, she wins, and of her harmonies
She is full sure! Upon her dying rose
She drops a look of fondness, and goes by,
Scarce any retrospection in her eye;
For she the laws of growth most deeply knows,
Whose hands bear here a seed-bag, there an urn,
Pledged she herself to aught, 't would mark her end!
This lesson of our only visible friend
Can we not teach our foolish hearts to learn?

. . . .

At dinner she is hostess, I am host.
Went the feast ever cheerfuller? She keeps
The Topic over intellectual deeps
In buoyancy afloat. They see no ghost.
With sparkling surface-eyes we ply the ball:
It is in truth a most contagious game;
HIDING THE SKELETON shall be its name.

Such play as this the devils might appal!
But here's the greater wonder; in that we,
Enamoured of our acting and our wits,
Admire each other like true hypocrites.
Warm-lighted glances, Love's Ephemeræ,
Shoot gaily o'er the dishes and the wine.
We waken envy of our happy lot.
Fast, sweet, and golden, shows our marriage-knot.
Dear guests, you now have seen Love's corpse-light
    shine!

. . . .

What are we first? First animals; and next
Intelligences at a leap; on whom
Pale lies the distant shadow of the tomb,
And all that draweth on the tomb for text.
Into this state comes Love, the crowning sun;
Beneath whose light the shadow loses form.
We are the lords of life, and life is warm.
Intelligence and instinct now are one
But Nature says: " My children most they seem
When they least know me; therefore I decree
That they shall suffer." Swift doth young Love
    flee;
And we stand wakened, shivering from our dream.

. . . .

How many a thing which we cast to the ground,
When others pick it up, becomes a gem!
We grasp at all the wealth it is to them;
And by reflected light its worth is found.
Yet for us still 't is nothing! and that zeal
Of false appreciation quickly fades.
This truth is little known to human shades,
How rare from their own instinct 't is to feel!
They waste the soul with spurious desire,
That is not the ripe flame upon the bough.

. . . .

Mark where the pressing wind shoots javelin-like
Its skeleton shadow on the broad-backed wave!
Here is a fitting spot to dig Love's grave;
Here where the ponderous breakers plunge and strike,
And dart their hissing tongues high up the sand:
In hearing of the ocean, and in sight
Of those ribbed wind-streaks running into white.
If I the death of Love had deeply planned,
I never could have made it half so sure,
As by the unblessed kisses which upbraid
The full-waked sense; or, failing that, degrade!

'Tis morning: but no morning can restore
What we have forfeited. I see no sin:
The wrong is mix'd. In tragic life, God wot,
No villain need be! Passions spin the plot:
We are betrayed by what is false within.

YOUNG REYNARD.

I.

GRACEFULLEST leaper, the dappled fox cub
Curves over brambles with berries and buds,
Light as a bubble that flies from the tub
Whisked by the laundry-wife out of her suds.
Wavy he comes, woolly all at his ease,
Elegant, fashioned to foot with the deuce;
Nature's own prince of the dance: then he sees
Me, and retires as if making excuse.

II.

Never closed minuet courtlier! Soon
Cub-hunting troops were abroad, and a yelp
Told of sure scent; ere the strike upon noon
Reynard the younger lay far beyond help.

Wild, my poor friend, has the fate to be chased,
Civil will conquer: were 't other 't were worse.
Fair, by the flushed early morning embraced,
Haply you live a day longer in verse.

MARTIN'S PUZZLE.

I.

There she goes up the street with her book in her hand
And her " Good morning, Martin ! " — Ay, lass, how d' ye do?
" Very well, thank you, Martin ! " — I can't understand !
I might just as well never have cobbled a shoe.
I can't understand it. She talks like a song;
Her voice takes your ear like the ring of a glass;
She seems to give gladness while limping along,
Yet sinner ne'er suffered like that little lass.

II.

First, a fool of a boy ran her down with a cart,
Then her fool of a father — a blacksmith by trade —
Why the deuce does he tell us it half broke his heart!
His heart! — where 's the leg of the poor little maid!
Well, that's not enough; they must push her down-stairs,
To make her go crooked: but why count the list?
If it's right to suppose that our human affairs
Are all ordered by Heaven — there bang goes my fist!

III.

For if angels can look on such sights — never mind!
When you 're next to blaspheming, it 's best to be mum.
The parson declares that her woes were n't designed;
But then, with the parson it 's all kingdom come.

Lose a leg, save a soul — a convenient text ;
I call it Tea doctrine, not savouring of God.
When poor little Molly wants 'chastening,' why, next
The Archangel Michael might taste of the rod.

IV.

But to see the poor darling go limping for miles
To read books to sick people ! — and just of an age
When girls learn the meaning of ribands and smiles !
Makes me feel like a squirrel that turns in a cage,
The more I push thinking the more I revolve :
I never get farther ; — and as to her face,
It starts up when near on my puzzle I solve,
And says, "This crushed body seems such a sad case."

V.

Not that she's for complaining : she reads to earn pence ;
And from those who can't pay simple thanks are enough.
Does she leave lamentation for chaps without sense ?
Howsoever, she's made up of wonderful stuff.

Ay, the soul in her body must be a stout cord;
She sings little hymns at the close of the day,
Though she has but three fingers to lift to the Lord
And only one leg to kneel down with to pray.

VI.

What I ask is, Why persecute such a poor dear,
If there 's Law above all? Answer that if you can!
Irreligious I 'm not; but I look on this sphere
As a place where a man should just think like a man.
It is n't fair dealing! But, contrariwise,
Do bullets in battle the wicked select?
Why, then it 's all chance-work! And yet, in her eyes,
She holds a fixed something by which I am checked.

VII.

Yonder riband of sunshine, aslope on the wall,
If you eye it a minute 'll have the same look:
So kind! and so merciful! God of us all!
It 's the very same lesson we get from the Book.
Then is Life but a trial? Is that what is meant?
Some must toil, and some perish, for others below;

The injustice to each spreads a common content.
Ay! I've lost it again, for it can't be quite so.

VIII.

She's the victim of fools; that seems nearer the
　　mark.
On earth there are engines and numerous fools.
Why the Lord can permit them, we're still in the
　　dark;
He does, and in some sort of way they're his
　　tools.
It's a roundabout way, with respect let me add,
If Molly goes crippled that we may be taught;
But perhaps it's the only way, though it's so bad;
In that case we'll bow down our heads, — as we
　　ought.

IX.

But the worst of *me* is that when I bow my head,
I perceive a thought wriggling away in the dust,
And I follow its track, quite forgetful instead
Of humble acceptance, for question I must!
Here's a creature made carefully — carefully made!
Put together with craft, and then stamped on, and
　　why?

The answer seems nowhere; it's discord that's
  played.
The sky's a blue disk! — an implacable sky.

X.

Stop a moment. I seize an idea from the pit:
They tell us that discord, though discord alone,
Can be harmony when the notes properly fit;
Am I judging all things from a single false tone?
Is the Universe one immense Organ that rolls
From devils to angels? I'm blind with the sight,
It pours such a splendour on heaps of poor souls.
I might try at kneeling with Molly to-night.

INDEX.

INDEX.

Accuracy of vision, 137.
Action, means life, 134.
Actions, we are now and then above them, 34.
Addle-pated, thinking many things, 24.
Aim, at stars, 75; man's, 103; at ideal life, 122.
Ale and Eve, 35.
Ambition, over sensitive, 166.
Ambitions, first, 36.
Anchor the heart, 12.
Anecdotes, 158.
Aphhorist reads himself, 24.
Aristocracy, worship of, 74.
Astronomers condescending, 134.
Audacity of expression, 49.
August, month of sober maturity, 166.
Autumn, the primrose blooms, 26.

Baggage, women in the rear, 124.
Beauchampism, 97.
Beauty, power in, 14; for the hero, 27; of laws, 89; is rare, 152.
Bone and marrow of study, 76.
Bone in a boy's mind, 99.
Books, peculiarity of, 99.
Bookworm women, 166.
Boys putting down ciphers, 72.
Brainless in art and statecraft, 134.
Burlesque Irishman, 153.

CHARACTER of a bullet, 25.
Characteristics of girls, 57.
Charity, Mrs. Berry's, 22.
Children think for themselves, 16; of wealth, 117.
Church, stands for drama, 109.
Cleopatra, 158.
Cleverness in a woman, 92.
Comedies, youth's tragedies, 37.
Comfort, religion of, 128.
Convictions, first impressions, 98.
Conventionalism, a dash of, 105.
Country, people of, 58; true to itself, 65.
Coward among us, 26.
Creed that rose in heaven, 125.
Critic, office of, 58.
Cynicism, intellectual, 86.

DANGER of little knowledge, 16.
Deathlessness in what we do, 57.
Debate in Baronet's mind, 19.
Desire to realize gains, 115.
Despair, wilful business, 53.
Devil, 167.
Digestion weak for wrath, 19.
Dinner, every, has its special topic, 37; gives good dinners, 147.
Dinner-tables, people at them, 85.
Disappointment, 51.
Drolleries like odors, 147.
Dyspepsy, 13.

EACH woman, Eve, 17.
Earnestness its own cure, 109.
Earth was not earth, 200.
Earth's secret, 200.
Eclipse, strange when the hue of truth, 85.
Education for women, 111.

English, middle class, 128, 129.
English women, 157.
Enthusiasm does not know monotony, 174.
Esteem 's a mellow thing, 93.
Eternal, sense of the, 146.
Experience of the priest in our country, 125.

FAMILIES, when worthy of veneration, 115.
Fate, attached to some women, 57.
February blew southwest, 182.
Fever, Carry your fever to the Alps, 80.
Fiction, shun those who cry out against it, 136.
Flattery of beholding a great assembly, 66.
Fools, compassion for them, 61 ; to be set spinning, 94.
Fortress, every one its weak gate, 10.
France, 210.

GIRL, Let a girl talk with her own heart, 37.
God of the world, 18.
Great-hearted Alvan, 138.
Green-tea talk, 168.

HEADS move a conspiracy, 65.
Heaven, to be close with, 204.
Heavens propitious to true lovers, 11.
Heights to right and left, 184.
Hero of two women, 93.
Heroes not in the habit of wording declarations of war, 23.
Heroics, "He's off in his heroics," 26.
Heroine in common with hero, 24.
Highly civilized natures, 48.
Honeymoon shining, 18.
Honeymoon Mahomet's minute, 19.
Hope and not be impatient, 72.
Hymeneal rumours, 171.

IDEAL of conduct for women, 87.
Ideas, language too gross for, 12.
Idols, critical of them, 19.
Imagination misled the old man, 61; pale flower of, 123.
Immeasurable love, 9.
Indigestion of wrath, 21.
Infants are said to have ideas, 177.
Irishmen like horses, 153.
Irresistible, the presence of the, 135.
Italian light, 135.

JEALOUSY of a woman is the primitive egoism, 90.
Jokes, good jokes not good policy, 178.
Judgments, men's, of women, 146.

KNOWLEDGE, danger of a little, 16.

LADY, manners of, 61.
Language of social extremes, 20; flowed from Renée, 112.
Language, how charged with it is a dog's tail! 177.
Laugh, promptness to, 21.
Letters, old, 59; of a lover, 101.
Life, 157, 174.
Light literature, 136.
London, 163.
Love, the blessed wand, 9; immeasurable, 9; the soul's ordeal, 11; the charioteer, 15; in a young girl, 37; and self-love, 38; the season of egoism, 87; slavery of, 112; old love reviving, 113; women read men by it, 123; strength in love, 136; and man, 139; to write of, 186, 187, 188.
Lover, letters of a, 101.
Lovers, heavens propitious to, 11; happy lovers, 11.

MAIDENS and their instincts, 89.
Makers of proverbs, 26.
Malice, barb of beauty, 53.

Man who speculates, 50; the laughing animal, 50; aim to culminate, 58; who looks on fallen women, 60; his review of life, 77; the strict man of honour, 91; who can be a friend, 92; a rough man, 121; for arbiter, 157.
Manners of a lady, 61.
Marriage, 154.
Matrimony, rosy and autumnal view, 15; Mrs. Berry's view, 25.
Men in most of us, 50; whose pride is their backbone, 86; who do not live in the present, 123; desire a still woman, 146; in the world, 156.
Men and women mysterious, 17; alike, 133.
Middle course, none for rich, 29.
Mind, consider sort of mind, 10; after oblivion, 169.
Minds of half-earnest men, 81.
Money, clothing for gentleman, 34.
Monsters, in politics, 150.
Moon surpassingly bright, 190.
Moral path, 169.
Mortals, silly sheep, 36.
Music, insensibility to it, 116.

NATURE, though heathenish, 13; speaks to Richard Feverel, 190, 191.
Nerve, touching a nerve, 37.
Nonsense of enthusiasts, 36.
Note in material fashions, 36.
Nothing but poetry makes romances possible, 179.

OBSERVATION an enduring pleasure, 157.
Opinions in packets, 154.

PAGAN, a virtue, 40.
Parasites complete the animal, 46.
Parsons and petticoats, 78.
Passion, strength in, 53.
Passive, in calamity, 21.
Pathos a tide, 91.

Peep-show, 152.
Philosophical geography, 16.
Philosophy, spirit of modern, 75; bids us see ourselves, 148; how may we know we have reached her, 148.
Pilgrim, he may be wrong, 17.
Pitch and tar in politics, 99.
Poetic and commonplace, 163.
Poetry, nonsense, 10; love, 11.
Poets and women, 173.
Power of resisting invasion, 163.
Pray, Can you pray? 50.
Prayer is good, 126.
Prayer, our prayers, 126; the fountain of prayer, 127.
Preacher, the born, 9.
Pride, the one developed faculty, 33.
Priests in our country, 125.
Professors, prophets, masters, each his creed, 125.
Projector of plots, 34.
Prose can paint evening, 163.
Puns the small-pox of language, 79.
Purpose wedded to plans, 34.

RADICALS marching to triumph, 114.
Rain had fallen, 182; after, 182.
Rare as an Epic song, 34.
Religion of England, 128.
Remarks have measured distances, 143.
Rich, love the nations, 120.
Ridicule, our own, knocks the strength out of us, 48.
Rubicon, it blew hard when Cæsar crossed, 15.

SAILING on a cruise is like, 122.
Science, Sir Austin looked at life as a, 11.
Selection can only be made from a crowd, 48.
Self-submerged, 53.
Sense of honour, 38.
Sentimental people, 145.

Sentimentalists seek to enjoy, 13; a natural growth, 45; like children, 49.
Service, noblest office on earth, 128; our destiny, 145.
Simplicity, 169.
Skill and care rescue a drowned wretch, 14.
Slumberers roused in darkness, 120.
Social sewerage, 23.
Song, rare as an Epic, 34.
Souls, weak souls, 138.
Speech, small change, 19; hauled from the depth, 33.
Strength in love, 136.
Struggle with society, 39.
Systems fortified by philosophy, 147, 186.

TEMPER. best-bottled, 71.
Think, Who can think and not think hopefully? 172.
Thirst not enjoyment, 122; for hopeful views, 162.
Tinkler, called piano, 103.
Titles, way to defend them, 100.
Truth, a rough, 93.

VALLEY, elevation above, 183.
Vanity chief traitor, 173.
Veterans in their arm-chairs, 58.
Vittoria read the faces of the mornings, 67.

WEALTH, children of, 117.
Women, each one an Eve, 17; a soft woman, 18; deeply bound to habit, 35; repose upon positive men, 46; seeking an anomaly, 59; make new spheres, 59; the noblest order of, 76; ideal for, 87; cowards, 91; of intellect, 92; tried and steadfast, 93; education for, 111; like to be loved, 111; artificial, 117; our awful baggage, 124; who can hold one back? 137; what a woman thinks of women, 143; conversationally, 144; men's opinion of, 146; judgments upon, 146 loneliness of, 146; motive life of, 147; and weather, 152; woman a mute, 154 hypocrites, 157; witty, 164.

Words big in the mouth, 93.
Work is medicine, 60; at people, 116.
World variable, 18; in motion, 119; ruthless, 156; of a fluid civilization, 157; imagination, 167.

YOUNG man who can look at fallen women with a noble eye, 60.
Young men and old men our hope, 162.
Youth, eating his heart, 33; called upon to look up, 47; soul of, 66.
Youths, like Pope's women, 33.

University Press: John Wilson & Son, Cambridge.

www.ingramcontent.com/pod-product-compliance
Lightning Source LLC
Chambersburg PA
CBHW022106230426
43672CB00008B/1295